SAVING THE Afterlife

II

More True Tales of a Paranormal Investigator

Ryan Dunn

Schiffer Publishing Ltd

4880 Lower Valley Road • Atglen, PA 19310

Designed by Danielle D. Farmer
Cover design by Matthew Goodman
Type set in Dead Secretary/Porcelain/Birch/Times

ISBN: 978-0-7643-5471-7
Printed in the United States of America

Published by Schiffer Publishing, Ltd.
4880 Lower Valley Road
Atglen, PA 19310
Phone: (610) 593-1777; Fax: (610) 593-2002
E-mail: Info@schifferbooks.com
Web: www.schifferbooks.com

For our complete selection of fine books on this and related subjects, please visit our website at www.schifferbooks.com. You may also write for a free catalog.

Schiffer Publishing's titles are available at special discounts for bulk purchases for sales promotions or premiums. Special editions, including personalized covers, corporate imprints, and excerpts, can be created in large quantities for special needs. For more information, contact the publisher.

We are always looking for people to write books on new and related subjects. If you have an idea for a book, please contact us at proposals@schifferbooks.com.

Other Schiffer Books by the Author:
Savannah's Afterlife: True Tales of a Paranormal Investigator
ISBN: 978-0-7643-4769-6

DEDICATION

*First and foremost, I would like to dedicate this book
to my Lord and Savior, Jesus Christ. Thank you for allowing
me to make a living doing what I love.
This has been an amazing journey; thank you for
being there every step of the way.*

This book is also dedicated to my amazing wife Kim Dunn; thank you for traveling into the world of the unknown with me—there is no one else I would want by my side.

To my beautiful daughters, Jennifer and Addison, thank you for making life worth living!

I also dedicate this book to the memory of my father, David Richard Dunn. Your time was cut way too short, but I will always cherish the memories we made while you were still here on earth.

Have a spooky little Christmas!

Ryan Dunn

CONTENTS

ACKNOWLEDGMENTS

This book would not have been possible without many people whom I owe a great deal of thanks. This is going to be a long list, and if I have forgotten anyone, I apologize. I tried my best to include everyone involved with this work. First and foremost, I would like to thank my Lord and Savior, Jesus Christ, who with Him all things are possible. A huge thanks to my beautiful wife Kim and my two daughters, Jennifer and Addison, for putting up with the long hours I put into writing this book. And to my lovable English Bulldog Griswold, who convinced me to take the necessary breaks from work to play fetch and tug of war. Thank you to Chef Mark Elliott and his wife Kelly for all of the support and guidance over the years. Thanks to my editor Guieneverre Cutlip for all of your work in editing the book, as well as my editors at Schiffer Publishing, Dinah Roseberry and Ian Robertson. Thank you again to Pete Schiffer for taking a chance on a new author.

I could not have done all the research without my team, the Savannah Ghost Research Society: Kim Dunn, spiritual specialist; Kris Kersten, photographer; and Shaun Holcomb, equipment tech. Thanks guys for your many hours put in on investigations and reviewing evidence. Also I owe a huge debt of gratitude to Josh Winters, Brand Harper, and Shaleena Twele of the Moon River Brewing Company for allowing us to investigate there frequently. I owe thanks to the ladies at the Georgia Historical Society for all of their assistance in my unending quest for historical data. Also thank you to Gwen and Kristina Kersten for all the support and help over the years with our research.

I also need to thank the people who allowed us overnight access to their properties to conduct all of the investigations that you are getting ready to read about. Thanks to Pedro Sarinana and his family for allowing us to investigate Juarez Restaurant, as well as Jose "Pollo" Rodriguez for taking the time to be interviewed about his experiences in the building. I owe appreciation to the Olde Pink House Restaurant staff—Meghan Littlefield, Jason Restivo, and Brian Friel—for their help letting us investigate there.

I can't thank Cathy Collasanto enough for allowing us overnight access to the Pirate's House Restaurant, and for Chad and his wife Kerry Valery for staying with us that night. To my neighbors Fred and Connie Hallaran, thank you for opening your home to us to investigate, you are the best neighbors anyone could ask for. The B&D Burgers on Congress Street investigation, as well as the Old Chatham County Jail investigation, would not have been possible without Gena Bilbo, Angela Lynn of Sixth Sense World® Historic Ghost & Cemetery Tours, and Kelly Spurlock, psychic medium. Also thanks to Corey Harper, Brian Counihan, and Russell Smith with the Chatham County Sheriff's Department for their help in the jail investigation.

In addition, Mindy Shea at the Savannah Chamber of Commerce was a huge help, putting me in touch with Sandra Baxter, who allowed us to investigate the Georgia State Railroad Museum, the Visitor's Center Museum on Martin Luther King Boulevard, and the Siege of Savannah Battlefield site. These sites, as well as Old Fort Jackson, are operated by the Coastal Heritage Society, that was more than gracious to allow us to investigate all of their locations. In addition, I must thank Brian Lee, Neil Moore, and Ray Christy for their invaluable knowledge of Old Fort Jackson and their willingness to let us research the fort.

To Tara Reese at Kevin Barry's Irish Pub, thank you for not only staying with us during the investigation, but for being brave enough to participate with us as well. I am also in debt to Susie Ridder, innkeeper of the Hamilton-Turner Inn, and Tim O'Byrne, the inn's concierge, for letting us be the first paranormal research team to investigate the property. To Tim Gardiner and the Congress Street Social Club staff, I really appreciate your patience with us during our late hours of investigating there. To Crazy Jim Hendricksen, my next door neighbor, I look forward to many more late nights in the courtyard drinking grog and lighting rocket fuel on fire.

Thanks to the entire staff of the Marshall House Hotel, as well as Jennifer Salandi at the Ballastone Inn for the investigation opportunity. John Nichols, Paige Brown, and Gail Lusk at the Crystal Beer Parlor, you all are the best! It was awesome to investigate one of our favorite restaurants in town. I owe appreciation to Maureen Craig, owner of Alligator Soul, and the restaurant's general manager Jason Johns for letting us in overnight to conduct our research. To Orlin Reynolds, former house tour director of the Sorrel-Weed House, your knowledge of the home was astonishing; I am so glad we finally got to investigate the home. Thanks to Bob and Michelle Masteller at Churchill's Pub for getting Andy Holmes to let us investigate there, not to mention being the two most amazing bartenders on the planet. To Scott and Kristen Haglund, Linsay Hubbard, and Stacie Gilbert, what a hell of a case! I am just glad the girls are out of that house.

In addition to the numerous thanks for everyone who allowed us access to the locations and helped with research, I need to thank all of the media for their coverage of our investigations. Thanks to WJCL-ABC News, WTGS FOX News 28, WSAV News, WTOC News, Karson Hoagland and the *Savannah Morning News*, Frank Sulkowski, and Russ Matthess at www.designingfear.com. Also many thanks to Jessica Leigh

Lobos and *Connect Savannah* newspaper, Jeremiah Johnson and the "Do" section of the *Savannah Morning News*, and Georgia Public Broadcasting Radio. As far as national networks, thanks to the folks at A&E's *My Ghost Story: Caught on Camera*, SyFy Channel's *Paranormal Witness*, and CMT's hit show, *Party Down South*. Also thanks to Nick Groff, Katrina Weidman, and Rob Saffi from Destination America's *Paranormal Lockdown* for allowing us to be a part of the show.

Last, but certainly not least, I would like to thank a few of those that have paved the way for the rest of us in the field of paranormal research. Thank you to Ed and Lorraine Warren, John Zaffis, Harry Price, Hans Holzer, Loyd Auerbach, and Sarah Estep, just to name a few. Also thanks to Gary Galka at Pro-Measure and Bill Chappell at Digital Dowsing for all of your inventions we use on every investigation, and to Shaun Porter at www.ghoststop.com for always having anything we need in stock. Thanks again everyone, I could not have done it without you!

Introduction

Before delving into Savannah's rich history and haunted past, I would like to take a few moments to introduce myself. My name is Ryan Dunn, and I am an author, paranormal investigator, and ghost tour owner in Savannah, Georgia—often referred to as "America's Most Haunted City." I moved to Savannah in 2010, with my wife and two young daughters to start a new chapter in our lives, but little did we know how it would change our lives forever. We moved into a haunted house in the historic district, and ever since we have been involved in the world of the paranormal. In the past six years we have established the Savannah Ghost Research Society, a non-profit organization that investigates hauntings and other ghostly phenomena. In addition, we opened Afterlife Tours in 2013, a walking ghost tour in Savannah's historic district that features real paranormal evidence at every location captured by our research team. We have been featured on A&E's *My Ghost Story: Caught on Camera*, and most recently on SyFy Channel's *Paranormal Witness* and CMT's *Party Down South*.

When I first set out to write this book, I was debating whether or not to include a chapter on Savannah's early history. Since this book is a sequel to my first, *Savannah's Afterlife: True Tales of a Paranormal Investigator*, I decided against it. In that book chapter 1 (Savannah's Tragic Past) is dedicated to just that. I did not want to rewrite something I had already written, so I decided instead to write even further into Savannah's early history through the tales that you are about to read and how that history applies to the hauntings in each location. If you would like to read even more about Savannah's earlier days I recommend reading some of the books mentioned in my bibliography, as they were paramount in the research involved for this book. In addition, every single story in this book has been fully researched at the Georgia Historic Society. Everything you are about to read is one hundred percent historically accurate, and we will be disproving some of the most famous stories in our city as the

The Georgia Historical Society, where we do all of
our historical research.

real dark past of Savannah unfolds. Let's just say that Savannah, being the thirteenth colony of the United States, as well as one of the largest slave-owning colonies, has had more than its fair share of tragedy. From Yellow Fever epidemics to slave trade and destruction by fire, this city has seen it all. Before we get started, I would like to take a brief moment to answer some questions that I am asked quite frequently—most often on my ghost tour.

The Savannah Ghost Research Society's current lineup, from left to right: Kris Kersten, Equipment Technician and Photographer; Ryan Dunn, Founder and Historian; Kim Dunn, Founder and Spiritual Specialist.

HOW DID YOU BECOME INTERESTED IN THE PARANORMAL?

When I was first asked this question a few years ago my answer was that I lived in a haunted house. After seeing the activity firsthand I developed an interest in trying to explain the unexplainable. After much thought, my involvement with the world of spirits began many years earlier. As early as first grade, I remember my father taking me to the school book fair. He bought me a copy of *Scary Stories to Tell in the Dark* by Alvin Schwartz, with illustrations by Stephen Gammell. As soon as I opened the book I was hooked. I spent the next few years reading that book over and over, and by fifth grade, I was reading the works of Stephen King, Anne Rice, Clive Barker, Edgar Allan Poe, and H. P. Lovecraft. By age seven, my father had introduced me to *Poltergeist II: The Other Side*, and to this day I still have a deep-rooted fear of Reverend Henry Kane, the film's ghostly villain. Over the years I have become an avid fan of horror films, and I have always had a penchant for the strange and unusual. Looking back, it makes complete sense as to how I found my way into this business, but I would not change it for the world. I get to do what I love for a living and there is nothing better than that.

WHAT ARE GHOSTS?

I am asked all the time, "What is a ghost?" This is a hard question to answer, because there are different types of hauntings, so just like people, every single case is completely different. There are similarities in every case, so we are able to classify these spirits into different types of hauntings.

Intelligent Haunting: An intelligent ghost is the type of ghost we have all come to know through popular culture. These are the spirits of those that have not yet crossed over. Some have chosen to stay behind, others are trapped here, and yet others are lost and have not found their way. These entities can communicate with the living, and in extreme cases can cause harm.

Residual Haunting: A residual haunting occurs when a tragic event happens and the event is somehow trapped in a never-ending loop. The best way to describe this is like a movie clip that replays itself over and over. Many residual hauntings are seen near old battlefields, such as Gettysburg, and other areas where grisly events took place. Many visitors to these places have reported seeing apparitions of soldiers who continue walking by, as if in a different period of time. These entities are not aware of us, and their spirit may have long since crossed over, but the apparitions continue to pass by, as if somehow trapped in time. When these tragic events happen, "the electrical impulses released by the brain during traumatic instances is somehow embedded in the moist rock on the grounds in which the event occurred." This is known as Stone Tape Theory, and was first developed by British archaeologist turned parapsychologist Thomas Charles Lethbridge. (Lethbridge, Thomas Charles. *Ghost and Ghoul: An Archaeologists Account of his Personal Experiences with the Supernatural.* Doubleday & Company, 1962)

Poltergeist Haunting: The term "poltergeist" is German for "noisy ghost." This is a loosely based term for any paranormal situation in which inanimate objects inexplicably move on their own. This can include chairs being stacked on tables, drawers being opened and shut by themselves, objects thrown through the air, loud unexplainable rapping on the walls, and many other such occurrences. In some poltergeist cases the objects are moved by spirits, while in others they have centered around teenagers. Many teenagers going through puberty have experienced poltergeists. The theory is that the angst of life changes in some teens has caused objects to move about on their own. Somehow the activity is centered around the teen, and when they become emotionally charged poltergeist activity occurs. These types of poltergeist cases usually only last a few months and then tend to cease, and in most instances like this the activity does not involve an angry spirit.

Portal Haunting: A portal haunting, or vortex haunting, is one of the most unusual types of hauntings. These exist where the haunted location happens to be near or on top of a portal or doorway from the spirit realm into our world. In a portal haunting, there are usually multiple entities from many different time periods coming and going. These are particularly dangerous because there is no telling what may pass through at any given time, and not all of these entities are friendly.

Demonic Haunting: A demonic haunting is definitely the most frightening type of haunting. Although some like to claim any activity that includes physical attacks, such as scratches and bite marks, as demonic, many of these instances can be attributed to a malevolent spirit. A demonic entity is one that never had a human soul to begin with. In Christianity, these were the fallen angels that joined Lucifer in his fall from Heaven. In these particular cases there tend to be many patterns of threes, including clocks in the home being turned back or set forward by three hours, knockings in groups of threes, and scratch marks appearing inexplicably in triplicate. This is evidence of a demonic entity, as it is mocking the Holy Trinity by doing these things in groups of three.

Although these five categories can describe most types of ghostly encounters, some cases have had multiple types of hauntings occurring at the same time. For instance, in most demonic hauntings poltergeist activity is known to occur.

HOW DO GHOSTS AND THE SPIRIT REALM AFFECT YOUR RELIGION?

I myself am Christian, and the first thing I wondered when I began to do ghost research was, "How does this tie in with the Bible?" Believe it or not, there is evidence of ghosts in numerous places in the Bible. For instance, in the book 1 Samuel, Chapter 28, Samuel came back as a ghost and spoke with Saul. In addition, in Luke 24, when Christ came back, his disciples thought he was a spirit, and he told them to touch him to see that he was indeed not a ghost. In these passages and others it is evident that in addition to Heaven and Hell there is also a spirit realm.

Throughout this book you will hear real tales of all manner of hauntings that occurred in the city of Savannah and the surrounding areas. Every story includes

The Savannah Ghost Research Society at their investigation of the Waverly Hills Sanatorium in Louisville, Kentucky. Pictured from left to right: Kris Kersten, Ryan Dunn, and former investigator Shaun Holcomb.

accurate history fully researched at the Georgia Historical Society, as well as personal accounts from the individuals that experienced these hauntings. In addition, you will hear what happened to our investigation team when we investigated these hauntings for ourselves. All real names have been used throughout the book, and no names were changed to protect privacy. Luckily, everyone was willing to let me use their real names when writing this book. As with my first book, this sequel is as real as it gets.

Happy Hauntings,
Ryan Dunn

NIGHT TERRORS
The Juarez Restaurant Investigation

The haunts at the Juarez Restaurant have been frightening the staff for years.

It is no secret that Savannah has its fair share of great places to eat, and Juarez Restaurant, at 420 East Broughton Street, is no exception. Sitting at the corners of Broughton and Price streets, Juarez has been serving up the best authentic Mexican cuisine in town for years. The name of the restaurant is a proud statement to the owner Pedro Sarinana's hometown Juarez, Mexico. The restaurant is well known for their traditional Mexican fare and fresh margaritas, but I had first heard about the hauntings at Juarez Restaurant in Al Cobb's *Savannah's Ghosts*. Ever since first reading his story on the restaurant I had wanted to investigate the place, and in September 2012,

I received the opportunity. Earlier in the year Guieneverre Cutlip had joined the team as our marketing director. Guien had been friends with Pedro and all of the folks at Juarez for years, so it did not take too much persuading for him to allow our team overnight access to his restaurant.

THE HISTORY

Before the existing building which now houses the Juarez Restaurant was built, there were two previous wooden structures that existed on the lot. These wooden homes were built in 1888, for a man named J. H. Entelman and the Burch Family Estate. In 1900, Herman H. Geffken acquired the property. Geffken and his wife Meta owned a grocery store and bar next door to the lot at 422 East Broughton Street. In 1909, the Geffkens built their family home on the lot where the two wooden structures existed, using part of the wooden buildings in the construction of their brick home. This new structure is now what stands at 420 East Broughton Street as the Juarez Restaurant.

The Geffkens continued to prosper for many years until Herman died of old age in the building in 1936. Mrs. Geffken continued to live in the home until she joined her husband six years later in 1942. Throughout the 1940s and early '50s John Pappadea, an employee at the Palace Luncheonette, lived in the home with his wife, Joanna. In 1955, Pete Gesson, an employee at Royal Bakery, acquired the property and lived there until the early '60s. After he left in 1961, Tom Pitsonis, another Royal Bakery employee, lived there until he retired in 1966. From 1967 to 1982, the building remained completely vacant, then in 1983, 420 East Broughton Street underwent extensive renovations and was later reopened that same year as the La Toque Restaurant, owned by Christian A. Bigler. La Toque thrived until the 1990s, then Pedro purchased the building and opened Juarez Restaurant in 1997.

THE HAUNTINGS

One of the biggest rumors tied to the restaurant is that the building had been previously used as an old firehouse, but there is no record that there was ever a fire station in the building. This story is quite possibly derived from the fact that when Pedro acquired the building in 1997, there were fire department-themed murals on almost every wall. In addition, they found a lot of fire department memorabilia. Perhaps the previous restaurant was firefighter-themed, but no one knows for sure from where these murals actually originated. During renovations Pedro had all of the murals painted over except for one; toward the back of the restaurant there is a mural that depicts a burning building with a dark shadowy figure trapped in the upper second story window. A fire truck is seen parked just outside the building as the firemen rush to fight the fire. For whatever reason Pedro and the painters felt compelled to leave this painting as it was. Although the depiction gave them chills, this painting can still be seen on the wall at Juarez today.

Because of strong empathic feelings, Pedro and the painters felt compelled to leave this one painting on the wall of the restaurant during renovations.

PHANTOM FOOTSTEPS

According to Pedro, strange occurrences began almost as soon as they started to renovate the place. One afternoon in 1997, not long after purchasing the property, Pedro and a few workers were on the main floor doing some general repairs. Not even an hour into their work they began to hear strange noises coming from above them on the second floor. It sounded as if there were numerous people above them walking around and talking. Knowing there was no one on the second floor and that they were the only ones in the building, they could find no rational explanation for these phantom noises.

Not long after the renovations were complete and Juarez Restaurant was opened employees began to mention to Pedro that the building may be haunted.

There were reports from staff of seeing unexplained shadows walking by, and the apparition of a young female has been seen on numerous occasions by employees and patrons. Other staff members have reported uneasy feelings in the basement, particularly in the supply closet. It is here that employees have experienced the overwhelming feeling of being watched by unseen eyes, and there always seem to be extreme cold spots in the room.

One of the most common incidents that occurs at Juarez concerns the light switches in the basement. On more than one occasion Pedro would arrive at work in the morning to open up the restaurant only to find that the basement lights had been left on. He questioned his staff, who adamantly declared they had turned the lights off after closing the previous night. After multiple times of this happening Pedro decided to check the security cameras to find the culprit. At around 3:00 a.m. on the security camera you can see the basement lights, which are on a dimmer switch, come on by themselves. No one is in the building at the time of the event, and there is no apparition, nor any other apparent cause for this phenomenon.

NIGHT VISITORS

One of the most unnerving experiences happened to one of Juarez's longtime employees, Jose Rodriguez, affectionately known as "Pollo" to his friends and fellow employees. A few years back, Pollo used to live upstairs in an apartment on the second floor of the restaurant. Late one evening Pollo awoke to a heavy pressure on his chest, and as he laid in bed he could not move. Although he was fully awake, something was preventing his limbs from moving. Standing directly above him, hovering mere inches from his face, was the apparition of a young female. She was wearing what appeared to be a dark gown, and she looked to be in her late twenties to early thirties. After a few seconds she stood up, turned around, walked a few feet away from the bed, and then quickly disappeared. This was not the only time that this strange incident has happened.

According to Pollo, others that have since lived in that upstairs apartment have reported having the exact same experience, even down to the description of the same female spirit. This rules out the logical idea that Pollo's experience was caused by sleep paralysis. Many people have unexplained paranormal encounters during sleep, especially upon falling asleep and upon waking up. It is believed that when we enter our dream state our mind becomes more open to the spirit world. Many skeptics argue that these paranormal experiences are caused by sleep paralysis, which exhibits many of the same symptoms.

Sleep paralysis occurs when someone either falling asleep or waking cannot speak or move. They are well aware of their surroundings, yet they cannot move their limbs. This is many times accompanied by horrific hallucinations and mild paranoia. This is a very real condition, and I do believe it can explain many of the incidents that some people believe to be a paranormal encounter. However, I do believe there have been some people that have had ghostly encounters that were simply written off as sleep paralysis. In Pollo's case it seemed to be a paranormal event, considering that multiple tenants over the years have described the exact same occurrence, as well as the exact same spirit.

THE INVESTIGATION

When we arrived at Juarez Restaurant one warm late September night in 2012, we knew right away that we were in for an interesting investigation. Upon entering the building we passed the kitchen staff, who was headed home for the evening after a long night of work. As they walked by us every one of them performed the sign of the cross and was frantically murmuring prayers. Jeremiah Johnson, a freelance writer for the *Savannah Morning News*, had just arrived to do a story on our team for the "Do" section of the paper as the kitchen staff went by. After noticing the kitchen staff's ominous reaction to our team's arrival he came over and introduced himself. He mentioned that although he could not stay for the entire investigation, he was interested in assisting in the initial base readings of the building.

ANGRY SPIRITS

We began unpacking our equipment, and right away an audio recorder we had just turned on caught our very first EVP (Electronic Voice Phenomena) of the night. We were in the main dining room, setting up our cameras, when Guien's audio recorder picked up an EVP that said, "I'm gonna get you." Apparently these spirits were not too thrilled about our presence in the building, and we had just arrived! Less than two minutes later the same recorder caught another EVP that sounded like the exact same voice as the previous EVP. This time the spirit growled, "Hear me!" The investigation had not yet begun and there was already spirit communication.

As we went through the building conducting initial readings of temperature, electromagnetic energy (EMF), and humidity, I decided to place stationary audio recorders in the rooms of the restaurant that tended to have the most activity. These recorders were to remain recording throughout the entire evening in hopes of catching even more audio evidence. As soon as I placed an audio recorder on a table on the main floor toward the back dining room area and turned it on an EVP was immediately captured that clearly said, "Break his hand."

Although it seemed there were a lot of malevolent EVPs as we were setting up, once the investigation got underway the activity in the building really seemed to pick up. A little over an hour into the investigation Guien and I were conducting an EVP session in the basement supply closet when all of a sudden our K2 EMF meter started spiking with unexplainably high levels of EMF readings, some reaching over twenty milligauss. These spikes occurred for the next thirty minutes or so before stopping completely. At the same time this anomaly was occurring the overall presence in the room was almost overwhelming. There was a heavy, dense feeling in the atmosphere. It felt as if there was more than one unseen presence in the room, and this presence was not happy with our being there at all.

A MOCKING ENTITY

Not only was there a strange presence in the supply closet, but it seemed the entire basement was riddled with paranormal activity. It was no wonder the employees did not like coming down there alone. Not only was the basement itself creepy, but we kept hearing strange noises down there the entire evening. At one point, while our team was seated at a table in the center of the basement dining area conducting an EVP session, we could hear what sounded like very heavy footsteps pacing angrily back and forth across the floor directly above us. Around the same time Guien began to feel very uncomfortable and started complaining of a sudden heavy feeling in the air. Ryan Reese, our photographer, and I started teasing Guien about being afraid and Guien jokingly said, "I hate you all." Right afterward a spirit voice was caught on audio recording that mockingly repeated Guien by saying, "Hate you all."

As the evening rolled on we had a few other strange experiences, including one EVP caught that encouraged us to "Preach." Perhaps this spirit was referring to the reaction of the kitchen employees to our arrival earlier in the night, or maybe it was referring to something else entirely. We may never fully know why the Juarez Restaurant is haunted, or why the spirits there choose to linger around and not cross over to the other side. There is one thing for sure, there are indeed verified hauntings that occur there quite regularly, and not all of those spirits are friendly in nature. Some actually seemed to be quite angry with the living. Unfortunately, after over twenty years of serving the community, the Juarez Restaurant closed in December 2015. This Savannah staple will surely be missed.

PRETTY IN PINK

The Olde Pink House Restaurant
Investigation

The Olde Pink House Restaurant, originally built for colonist and slave owner James Habersham Jr. in 1771.

While strolling through the beautiful squares throughout Savannah's Historic District, you would be hard-pressed to find many structures that have stood the test of time as long as the Olde Pink House. Although Savannah was settled in 1733, much of our historic district was destroyed due to multiple fires, most notably the Great Fire of 1820. This fire consumed 463 structures before finally being extinguished. The Olde Pink House is one of the few structures that has survived every single fire that burned through our city over the years. Well known for its fabulous food and charming atmosphere, this restaurant has been a Savannah staple since its opening in 1971. The building dates to 1771, but our story starts much earlier, with the arrival of James Habersham to Savannah in 1738.

THE HABERSHAM FAMILY

James Habersham left England in 1738, to begin a fresh start in the new colony of Georgia. He came to aid his good friend George Whitfield, who had recently established the Bethesda Orphanage just outside the city. In 1740, he married his wife, Mary Bolton, in Bethesda, with George Whitfield presiding as priest. In 1744, he established a partnership with Col. Francis Harris, and the two opened the house of Harris and Habersham—the first commercial enterprise established in Georgia. A large import and export business, they developed trade routes to the colonies in the north, England, and the West Indies. Habersham later served as King Secretary of the Province and as President of the King's Council.

Although slavery was originally illegal in the colony of Georgia, by the year 1750, the ban was lifted. Soon afterward James Habersham had developed three rice plantations south of the city: Dean Forrest Plantation, Silk Hope Plantation, and Beverly Plantation. He was documented as having over 200 slaves, with his land totaling over 15,000 acres.

James and Mary had three sons: James Habersham Jr., Joseph Habersham, and John Habersham. James and his three sons were all Freemasons and members of the Solomon's Lodge in Savannah. While the father was an avid loyalist to the British crown, all three sons later played a big part in shaping our new nation during the American Revolution. Although a large rift was created between father and sons, James Habersham is still interred in a family crypt at Colonial Park Cemetery with all three of his sons.

John Habersham, the youngest of the three, served in the Revolutionary War as first lieutenant and brigade major of the First Georgia Continental Regiment, and later served as a member of the Continental Congress. He was captured twice by the British during the war: once in Charleston and once in Savannah. Later, during the 1790s, he was appointed by President George Washington as the port collector for Savannah.

Joseph Habersham, the middle son, was the one who gained the most fame during his lifetime. Joseph served as a colonel in the Continental Army during the Revolutionary War. At age twenty-three Joseph, along with Dr. Noble W. Jones, Edward Telfair, and a few others, raided a British powder magazine and stole 600 pounds of powder. After the war Joseph served as Postmaster General of the United States under Presidents George Washington and John Adams, later retiring under President Thomas Jefferson. After retiring, he later became the first president of the Savannah branch of the Bank of the United States. Joseph died in 1815; Habersham County, Georgia, was later named after him.

Although his two brothers fought on the continental side for American independence, it was James Habersham Jr. who stayed home during the war and helped to finance the patriot cause. In 1771, construction began on what is now known as the Olde Pink House Restaurant. It was originally built for James Habersham Jr., but the home was not completed until 1789, due to the Habershams' involvement in the American Revolution. After the war he became Speaker of the General Assembly in the years 1782 and 1784. He lived in the home for almost ten years until his death in 1799.

ANOTHER COLOR

It is said that the house's pink hue came from Mr. Habersham having his brick home covered with white stucco. The brick soon bled through the stucco, turning his house pink. After numerous attempts at repainting the home white the brick continued to bleed through. Now the house is painted pink, but this is supposedly where the color originated from. Whether it be truth or urban legend, it still makes for a great explanation.

Another story about the Pink House that I have heard for numerous years is that its original owner, James Habersham Jr., committed suicide by hanging himself in the basement of the home. The story has been told on many ghost tours and has been written in numerous haunted stories about the building. As my good friend and author James Caskey points out in his 2013 edition of his book *Haunted Savannah: America's Most Spectral City*:

> The erroneous story is that he learned of his wife's affair with the architect of the building and committed suicide. The truth is less theatrical, yet much more uplifting: the junior Habersham was a Revolutionary War financier, successful businessman, loving husband, and beloved father. His is the story of American triumph over adversity. Habersham died in 1799, and the cause of death is listed as "declining health." Burial of someone who had committed suicide was not permitted in consecrated ground, so the fact that James Habersham is buried with his father and brothers in Colonial Park Cemetery is yet another indicator that the story of his self-hanging is false.

HISTORY OF THE HOME

After the home's completion it was considered one of the first mansions in Savannah. Although smaller in size, the Pink House had a kitchen in the basement, one of the first homes in the city to have a kitchen in the home. Prior to that kitchens were kept in a structure behind the home, separate from the house itself. Many fires broke out in early kitchens, so these beautiful Victorian mansions were kept separate to avoid burning them down. Although most of the Habershams' two hundred plus slaves were south of the city at one of their three plantations, many of the women and children slaves were housed in the basement of this house to tend to the kitchen. The ghosts of these slaves are still witnessed on a regular basis in the basement of the Pink House, which is now the restaurant's tavern.

After James Habersham Jr.'s death in 1799, the building became the Planter's Bank of Georgia. Guests to the restaurant can still dine at a table in the old bank's vault to this day, which is now the restaurant's wine cellar. In 1865, Brig. Gen. Louis York used the home as a headquarters during the Union Army's occupation of Savannah. By the early 1900s, it was used as a lawyer's office, a real estate office, and an architect's office. By 1930, it became the Georgia Tea Room, ran by a Miss Alida Harper. In 1971, the building underwent full renovations and reopened in the fall of that year as the Olde Pink House Restaurant, under which it still operates to this day.

Since its reopening in 1971, there have been literally hundreds of reports of strange occurrences in the building. According to Meghan Littlefield, a manager at the Pink House, guests have left in the middle of dinner because they have seen the apparitions of slaves in shackles walking through the very walls in the basement. Others have seen strange apparitions walking the upstairs halls, and the ghost of James Habersham Jr. apparently likes to keep an eye on things as well; numerous guests and employees have seen him roaming throughout the building on several occasions.

The vault in the basement of the Olde Pink House was originally used as a bank vault, but has since been converted into the restaurant's wine cellar.

THE BASEMENT

Although paranormal activity has occurred on every floor of the old mansion, the tavern area in the basement tends to be the most active spot. One evening, a server's assistant who was delivering food in the tavern area had a very unnerving experience. He happened to look in the mirror across the bar and witnessed the apparition of a slave in tattered clothes staring back at him in the mirror. Most disturbing was the fact that the apparition was standing right behind him!

One of the most unexplainable occurrences in the building happens in the women's restroom in the basement. Although the locks on the doors there have been changed dozens of times, women still get locked in the restroom and can't get out. During one of these instances a young lady was locked in there for over fifteen minutes. When she finally became free she was covered in tears and visibly shaken by her experience. Evidently, she had gone into the bathroom some fifteen minutes earlier, and after she turned on the light switch and locked the door she saw the switch click out by itself and it all went downhill from there. She frantically tried to turn on the switch but it would not work. She unlocked the door but the handle would not turn. A few seconds later, she began to hear the sounds of little girls laughing at her coming from within the bathroom, yet she was the only one in there. A few moments afterward these little girls were telling her to "Get out" and to "leave." After she finally got out of the restroom she quickly exited the building and never returned.

Another thing that occurs quite often is that the fire alarms in the building will inexplicably go off by themselves. One night, after all of the guests had left, Service Manager Meghan Littlefield and a few others were closing up. The fire alarms began going off, so Meghan raced to the back office to check the security cameras. When she looked at the hallway camera there was a smoky apparition manifesting in the middle of the hall. Meghan was able to record this footage on her camera phone, and it has since been uploaded to YouTube with over 128,000 views.

Brian, one of the servers at the Pink House, had a strange occurrence with a family he was waiting on at table 32 in the front dining room. As with most haunted places in Savannah, the family was asking Brian about the ghosts of the Olde Pink House. As he was telling them a story the pigtails of the little girl sitting at the table lifted up on either side by themselves. It was as if someone was lifting her hair high into the air, yet no one was there. The family quickly paid for their appetizer course and decided to finish dinner somewhere else.

THE INVESTIGATION

In October 2012, I was contacted by Jessica Leigh Lobos, a reporter for *Connect Savannah*, a local newspaper. They wanted to do a story on us for Halloween, so we invited her to join us on an investigation at the Olde Pink House Restaurant. I arrived just after 11 p.m. that night with our investigators Guieneverre Cutlip and Ryan Reese. We met Jessica downstairs in the old tavern and sat by the roaring fireplace to discuss the night's investigation. After the guests had all filed out of the building we began to conduct our research, and it wasn't long before strange things began to happen.

As I was conducting initial base readings in the vault I heard Guien screaming from all the way down the hall. I raced down the hall and she was pointing at a row of chairs that lined the basement hallway. "He was just right there!" she exclaimed. A moment before, as she rounded the corner, Guien had seen the apparition of an older man seated in one of the chairs, holding his head in his hands. Later believed to be the ghost of an old slave, he looked up at Guien briefly and then quickly disappeared. We later captured two EVPs in that same area of a male entity whispering, "Help." About an hour later, in that same hallway, an EVP was captured of a woman who whispered, "That man looks like he's sleeping here." Could this woman be referring to the strange man Guien had witnessed a few hours earlier?

Later in the evening we were allowed access to the attic of the building, which we were not even expecting. Having the opportunity to see the hand-hewn timber and dovetail joints that framed the old house was absolutely amazing. Seeing the infrastructure in the attic really put into perspective how old this building was. While up there I decided to conduct a brief EVP session, and it was not long before I received a very clear response. I had asked: "Why are you still here? Why do you still haunt this place?" A male entity clearly replied, "The pain." The clarity of this EVP was absolutely chilling, because it actually sounded like this spirit was in a great deal of pain by the sound of his voice.

At around 4:45 a.m., as our investigation came to a close, I captured one of the most disturbing pieces of evidence that I have heard to this day. Everyone was going throughout the building, packing up all of the equipment. We were due to be out by 5:00 a.m., so we were finally wrapping things up. I was walking past the basement bathroom door, getting ready to break down an infrared camera and tripod. As I passed the women's restroom my audio recorder picked up a chilling EVP of a little girl that said, "Kill him." Since I was the only one in the basement at the time I could only assume this entity was referring to me. The last guests had left the building some five hours before and there were no kids locked in the house with us that night—at least not living.

The Olde Pink House Restaurant has some of the best food in town, and I would put it at the top of the list should you visit our great city. Their wine list, hand-selected by Sommelier Jason Restivo, is the most extensive in the city. Be sure to check out the basement, otherwise known as Planters Tavern, where there is live jazz most nights of the week. As for any females that do not wish to deal with the haunted restrooms, there are other facilities on the main floor that do not tend to have any strange activity.

DEAD MEN DO TELL TALES

The Pirate's House Restaurant
Investigation

The Pirate's House Restaurant sits on one of the oldest sections of Savannah's original colony and is considered one of the oldest standing structures in Savannah.

On the far east corner of Savannah's famed Historic District sits the Pirate's House Restaurant. This building is one of the oldest standing structures in the city, and the land itself dates to the earliest days of the colony. A must-see while visiting our beautiful city, this building has enthralled historians and paranormal researchers for many years. With the building being as old as it is, many facts about the place have been misconstrued over the years of its existence. But before we get that far, let's start from the beginning, when our first colonists landed on the bluff in early 1733, and established Savannah as the thirteenth colony.

TRUSTEES' GARDEN

Soon after arriving here, our colonists realized the need for farming and agriculture. The Trustees' Garden was established on the northeast corner of the bluff, which is where the Pirate's House now sits today. A ten-acre plot, the Trustees' Garden was an experimental garden in which medicinal herbs, coffee, spices, hemp, fruit trees, and many other things were grown. It has even been said that George Whitfield, founder of the Bethesda Orphanage, wrote many of his sermons while occasionally strolling through the gardens. Unfortunately, many of these crops failed due to Savannah's drastic climate, but peach trees and pecans were two of the most successful, for which Georgia is still well known to this day.

FORT WAYNE

On the far corner of the bluff, a very short distance from the Pirate's House, sits the ruins of old Fort Wayne. As soon as James Oglethorpe arrived with our very first colonists, he realized that we needed a fortification to protect the city. By 1734, Fort Halifax was completed, with "a battery on the river . . . beside them which two block houses at the angles of the town had each four guns . . .," according to Hugh McCall in *The History of Georgia*. In 1757, the fort was shown to have been equipped with a twelve pounder cannon. In 1760, the colonists decided to create an artificial hill on the bay near the fort. When the location was dug out the colonists discovered a large pile of human bones, leading to the area being nicknamed "Indian Hill." Since the colonists had just recently arrived here a few years prior in 1733, they believed these to be Native America REMains. Oglethorpe then approached Tomochichi, chief of the Yamacraw Indians, to apologize for disturbing the burial mound. The chief informed Oglethorpe that these were not Yamacraw bones, so these skeletons even predated the natives that were there when the colonists first arrived.

The fort was abandoned for many years to follow, then it was rebuilt by the patriots as "Fort Savannah" in 1776, and was later renamed "Fort Prevost" by the British, who captured it in 1779, when they attacked Savannah during the Revolutionary War. After the British evacuated the city, the fort was then named "Fort Wayne," which it is still called today. The fort was partially rebuilt in 1812, and it still exists to this day at the corner of Bay and East Broad Streets.

FOLEY'S ALLEY

Around 1753, the Trustees' Garden was redeveloped into a residential area, where homes and taverns were built. This area was known as "Foley's Alley"; it was the poor Irish section of town, and most definitely not the kind of place you wanted to be after dark. The building which now houses the Pirate's House Restaurant at 20 East Broad Street is said to be as old as 1753, but historic records show the building dating to 1794, when George Adam Kehler, a butcher, bequeathed the land to his grandson, John Adam Kehler. There are two parts to the structure: the Pirate's House and the Herb House. The Herb House was named after the area where the gardener for the Trustees' Garden would have lived and worked, though the structure was built much later. Although it is said to be the oldest building in Savannah, the Chart House Restaurant's building dates to 1791, and the James Habersham home, which houses the Olde Pink House Restaurant, was completed in 1789, both beating the Pirate's House by a few years.

Throughout the 1800s, the building was owned by several families and also served as a tavern, eventually being split into separate apartments by the 1900s. In 1941, it became the Pirate's House Museum, and in 1950, it became the Pirate's House Restaurant, which it remains to this day. The upstairs was a bar for many years called "Hard Hearted Hannah's," where Savannah songstress and "Lady of 6,000 Songs" Emma Kelly performed regularly. In 1945, the Savannah Gas Company acquired the property including the Pirate's House, Herb House, Trustees' Garden, and old Fort Wayne. Hansell Hillyer, the gas company president, left the extensive seven-year renovation project to his wife, Mary Hillyer, who saved all of the buildings from demolition and restored them to their original splendor. If not for the Hillyer's dedication to historic preservation the Pirate's House and the Fort Wayne area may have been completely destroyed.

SHANGHAIED

For many years tales of pirates have been tied to the building. There are stories that pirates used to frequent the place, and that unsuspecting sailors at the bar were "shanghaied," or forced into piracy. This would occur when the sailor was either slipped a drug in his drink or rapped over the head with a heavy blunt object. Supposedly they were dragged through tunnels which lead from the basement of the structure to the Savannah River. Ships waiting in the harbor would then sail into the night with their newly acquired captive. The following morning, the sailor would awake disoriented and out to sea. He would then be given a choice to either serve as a pirate for a few years or be thrown overboard into the middle of the ocean. Most chose the former, not the latter. There are even rumors that Blackbeard visited the place a few times.

There are a few discrepancies with this. According to historian John Fiske, the "Golden Age of Piracy" lasted from around 1650 to about 1720. With Savannah being settled with its first colonists much later in 1733, this was not possible. Although there may have been a few pirates here and there, most had been either captured or killed by then. As far as Blackbeard, he was killed on November 22, 1718, near Ocracoke Island by Lt. Robert Maynard of the HMS *Pearl* and his crew. According to Maynard, after examining Blackbeard's corpse, he reported that he had been "shot five times and cut twenty." Blackbeard's head was then hung from the mast of Maynard's ship. Once again, the years do not match up. If Blackbeard did indeed visit Savannah, there would have been no settlers at that time, just the Yamacraw Indians.

Regarding the practice of "shanghaiing," I did discover evidence of this occurring a few times in Savannah over the years. Although piracy was pretty much eradicated by the 1720s, a new threat existed on the high seas. Privateers, who were much more dangerous than pirates, were on the rise, and they were documented as visiting Savannah's ports on more than one occasion. A privateer was commissioned by a government by letters of marque to attack other ships during wartime. Not only were they strikingly similar to pirates, privateers had a whole government backing them! Since "Pirate's House" has a better ring to it than "Privateer's House," it makes sense as to how the structure received its moniker. Of all the privateers in history, Henry Morgan and Jean LaFitte are probably two of the most notorious. I found two separate occasions in Savannah's historical archives where privateer ships were attempting to "shanghai" Savannah citizens.

The first account was the sad story of William O. Golding, who was kidnapped at the Savannah waterfront at an early age. On July 15, 1882, an eight-year-old Golding was walking along the wharf in Savannah with his cousin when they passed a large ship called *The Wandering Jew*. As they passed by the ship, young William overheard the ship's captain, William Potter, say to his wife, Polly, "Pick one of those boys there." William was then invited aboard the ship, but by the time he realized what was going on it was too late. In 1932, in a letter written many years later by a much older William Golding to a Margaret Stiles, he recalled seeing the Tybee Island Lighthouse in the distance as the ship set out for sea. Golding met Stiles during his long stay at the Marine Hospital in Savannah, where he was treated for a lung condition. It was then that he began to recount his tales of his life on the sea to Stiles, where he served for nearly fifty years on several different ships.

LA VENGEANCE AND LA FRANCHISE

Many years before the Golding incident, on the evening of November 11, 1811, two French privateer ships—*La Vengeance* and *La Franchise*—were docked in Savannah's harbor. They were looking for new recruits and got into a scuffle with Savannah citizens. According to the *Columbian Centinel* in an article published on November 14, 1811:

> From Savannah–On Thursday evening last about 60 French privateersmen belonging to *La Vengeance* and other picaroons, which to the disgrace of

our administration, are permitted to skulk into and refit in our harbors, collected near their rendezvous, and being armed with long knives, sallied forth and attacked about 20 American seamen, when the mate of the brig *Hetty* of Philadelphia was stabbed in the heart, and instantly expired.

The young man mentioned who was killed was nineteen-year-old Jacob B. Taylor, whose headstone—describing in detail the cause of his death—is still mounted along the back wall of Colonial Park Cemetery. Soon after, the citizens of Savannah rallied together in a mob and set fire to the two French ships docked in the harbor.

Although there is no evidence that the tunnels underneath the Pirate's House were used for the purpose of "shanghaiing," we do know for a fact that this practice occurred on more than one occasion in Savannah.

One other well-known tale told about the Pirate's House is that of the ghost of Capt. Flint, who supposedly died in the upstairs bedroom, as mentioned in Robert Louis Stevenson's famed *Treasure Island*. Although the Pirate's House looks like it came right out of the book, the story was a work of fiction. Interestingly enough, in the book Flint was said to have died in Savannah shouting, "Darby M'Graw—fetch aft the rum," so it is understandable how this connection was made.

THE HAUNTINGS

For numerous years the Pirate's House Restaurant has been synonymous with hauntings. For quite a while our team (the Savannah Ghost Research Society) had been trying to gain overnight access to the building. One afternoon, I received a call from Frank Sulkowski, the sports director and assistant news director for WJCL-ABC News and WTGS-FOX News 28 in Savannah. It had been a while since we had filmed our series entitled *Spooky Town*, and Frank was ready to film our fourth episode. We spoke to the management at the restaurant and they finally agreed to let us in to film. I sat down one fall afternoon with one of the managers, Chad Valery, who spoke to me in detail about the paranormal activity in the building.

"I never feel alone in this place," said Chad, "even when I am the only one here locking up, I can feel someone constantly watching me." According to Chad, the Herb House, Rum Cellar, and the upstairs tend to be the most haunted areas of the building. Many employees refuse to enter the Rum Cellar, and many others report uneasy feelings there. Employees have also reported hearing heavy boot steps treading back and forth upstairs above them as they are closing up when no one else is in the building. Being such a busy restaurant, according to Chad, it seems that most of the activity would occur after all of the guests had left and everyone was closing up the building.

A GHASTLY ENCOUNTER

One evening, a female manager was closing up for the night and was the last one in the building. This was in the 1990s, when the back area of the restaurant used to be divided into separate dining rooms known as "95 South." The manager was walking down the hall past those dining rooms when all of a sudden a small ball came rolling out of one of the rooms past her feet. She thought it strange, but locked the ball in the office and went back to closing down the restaurant. She went to use the restroom, and as she was seated in the stall the same ball that she had locked in the office came rolling under the stall door. That manager promptly quit the following day.

On another occasion, a female manager was closing up for the night and she was the last one in the building. She noticed a small boy standing in the Herb House dining room. She thought maybe one of the guests had left their child behind and she became concerned for the young child. As she approached him to ask if he was lost the boy quickly disappeared. A while later a guest snapped a picture one afternoon in the Herb House during lunch and captured the apparition of a small boy on the stairs. He has been seen in the building quite a few times since then.

One night, a young couple was having dinner in the Captain's Room when they began to argue. Their incessant fussing escalated until other guests in the room were beginning to feel uncomfortable. All of a sudden a coffee filter holder from a coffee pot on the other side of the room flew across and struck the woman who was arguing in the back. It seemed the ghosts of the Pirate's House were fed up with the couples' racket. After sitting with Chad for over an hour, I knew that we were in for a great night of filming.

THE INVESTIGATION

On November 5, 2012, we arrived at the Pirate's House after closing to meet Frank Sulkowski and Biff Flowers, his cameraman, for the investigation. As soon as we arrived we began to unpack, while Frank went walking through the building to scope things out. Not two minutes after he left us Frank returned. "You're not going to believe what just happened!" exclaimed Frank. Frank had been walking in the dining room adjacent to Flint's Hall when he witnessed a dark apparition pass in front of a table and quickly disappear towards the kitchen. As he quickly exited the dining room, he noticed that the kitchen door the apparition was headed towards was swinging back and forth, as if something had just walked through it, yet he was the only one back there. We had just arrived and we were already experiencing activity! The back hallway area later proved to be highly active throughout the night. Later that evening Biff heard an unexplainable growling in his camera mic and phantom footsteps racing up behind him in this same area.

The Captain's Room also produced some great results. During an EVP session there we were receiving unexplainable high EMF fluctuations on our meters in response to our questions for nearly ten minutes. Also we caught a great Class A EVP in Captain Flint's Dining Room that said, "They're sitting here listening." We had been quiet for almost a whole two minutes when this one was captured, presumably talking about us. One of the saddest pieces of evidence captured that evening was in the Herb House of a small voice saying, "It hurts." Could this be the ghost of the child that the manager witnessed that evening?

The most disturbing piece of evidence was captured in the upstairs unfinished area of the building. I was up there with our photographer, Ryan Reese, filming when I said: "If you want us to leave, tell us." On the playback my audio recorder captured an EVP of a male spirit replying, "You just walk on home." Evidently it wanted us out of the building, and it sounded none too happy with me whatsoever. Later that evening I had to go to the car for some more equipment. Everyone else on the investigation stepped outside as well to get some fresh air. As soon as we shut the door and went outside, one of our stationary audio recorders that we had left in the building captured the clear voice of a female who said, "Goodbye." Evidently this entity thought we were leaving for the night!

Having the opportunity to be one of the only paranormal research teams to ever investigate the Pirate's House was a privilege, and the evidence we managed to capture was quite compelling. Not only is the Pirate's House famous for its hauntings, but it boasts some of the best southern cuisine in Savannah. A trip to our city is never complete without a trip to the Pirate's House for lunch. They serve some of the best homemade biscuits and corn muffins in town, and be sure to try a cup of their famous she-crab soup; they make some of the best in the city.

THE HALLARAN CASE

The 302 West Waldburg Street Investigation

The owners at 302 West Waldberg Street began to have experiences as soon as they bought the place.

I have spent years investigating the most famous haunted locations in Savannah and the surrounding area with my team, but it is the private residence cases that never cease to amaze me. These are usually unsuspecting homes that you may never guess to be haunted, but as they say, "You can't judge a book by its cover." In early 2013, I was approached by Fred and Connie Hallaran, who literally live just around the corner from me in the Historic District. The Hallarans had been dealing with paranormal activity in their home since purchasing the place in 2007, and they were interested in getting some answers.

THE HISTORY

The house, which was one of the first homes built on the street, was built in 1888, for a clerk named Thomas M. Keller. A few years later George Wiggins, a bookkeeper at T. West & Company, purchased the home with his wife Katie. The Wiggins lived there until 1914. In 1915, Wolf and Fannie Miller moved into the home. The Millers owned W. Miller & Son, a wholesale produce and poultry business in City Market. Wolf died in the home three years later in 1918, and Fannie later passed away there of old age in December 1952. By the 1960s, the home had been split up into two apartments, then it remained vacant throughout the early 1990s. As soon as the Hallarans purchased the place in 2007, strange activity began to happen. According to Fred, "The strange occurrences started the very day we bought the place!"

As soon as they had moved in Connie began to hear loud rapping on the walls near the stairwell and throughout the entire house. It was as if someone was pounding on the walls, yet she could find no explanation for the strange sound. Items were knocked off shelves by themselves, and things seemed to fall over for no apparent reason. On numerous occasions Connie has seen shadows dart past her out of the corners of her eyes. Many times Connie and Fred have felt strange cold spots and the overall feeling of being watched, even when they are completely alone.

A few weeks before our investigation Connie had an unnerving experience in the hallway. She was down on her knees, changing her cat's litter box, when she felt a soft hand touch her ankle. Thinking it was Fred she turned around, only to see that there was no one else in the hallway. Unlike the majority of the private residence cases we handle, the Hallarans did not feel threatened by the spirits in their home; they just wanted to know who may be haunting their house and why they were still there.

THE INVESTIGATION

It was just after dusk one cold February evening in 2013, when my wife Kim and I arrived at the Hallaran house to conduct our investigation. During our initial base readings we noticed some relatively high natural EMF (electromagnetic field) spikes which could account for some of the activity in the home. Ghosts are drawn to electromagnetic energy like a moth to a flame; it is what they use to manifest themselves. This energy can be found in electronics and many things we use today, such as everyday household appliances, light switches, and pretty much anything that uses electricity. When high EMF fields are present they can attract these spirits. In addition, high unexplainable EMF readings can also be a sign of the presence of a ghost.

As far as EVPs—or audio recordings of the dead—we managed to catch quite a few very clear ones. While in the downstairs hallway Kim asked, "Who knocks over things in this house?" A very clear voice responded, "I do." We received a similar answer later that evening while conducting an EVP session in Fred's office, which used to be the bedroom in which Mrs. Miller died in 1952. I asked, "Who made those loud knocks on the stairs?" A female entity responded, "Me." This very well could have been the spirit of Mrs. Miller still enjoying the home in which she had spent so many years of her life. One piece of evidence that led us to believe that the spirits in the home were not unhappy was also caught in Fred's office. Kim asked, "Are you stuck here?" An entity then responded, "Not anymore."

In addition to some great audio evidence, we were also able to document a few significant temperature drops, especially in Fred's office. This coincided with the reports from Connie and Fred of feeling strange cold spots throughout their home. Toward the end of the investigation Kim and I heard the strange knocking noises near the stairwell. We looked all about to find a rational explanation for these strange sounds to no avail. Evidently these spirits were trying to make themselves known to us.

After we wrapped up the investigation we spent the rest of the evening having a few cocktails with our neighbors, who were the most gracious of hosts. Fred had quite a few interesting stories to tell; he is definitely the type of guy that you could sit and listen to for hours. After retiring from the service Fred had worked his way up to become Senior Vice President of the Beverly Hills Savings Bank. Over the years he had handled loans for the likes of Johnny Carson and Charles Bronson, just to name a few. Not to mention Fred still receives a yearly Christmas card from longtime friend Grace Slick of Jefferson Airplane.

It was quite late into the evening when we finally said our goodbyes, but we were in need of some rest after the investigation. Not only were we able to walk away with some phenomenal evidence, but that night we gained two great friends, as well. Fred and Connie Hallaran still experience strange occurrences in their home on a regular basis, but theirs is a rare case in which they are able to coexist with the spirits that inhabit their home. Whether it is the ghost of Mrs. Miller or someone else entirely, the Hallaran home has its fair share of ghostly activity.

CHAPTER 5

THE RESTLESS DEAD

The B&D Burgers on Congress Street Investigation

Video evidence from the hauntings at B&D Burgers on Congress St. aired on *Good Morning America* in April 2013.

In late April 2013, the B&D Burgers Restaurant on Congress Street aired on *Good Morning America*. A security camera in the restaurant's basement had captured what appeared to be a strange paranormal occurrence. A stack of glass racks sitting against the wall went toppling over by themselves, as if pushed by some unseen force. There was no air flow or anything else around that may have caused the disturbance, and evidently, this strange video clip caught the attention of the national news. The following morning we received a phone call from Josh Colwell of WJCL-ABC News and WTGS-FOX News 28 in Savannah. Being that we film quite often with them, Frank Sulkowski, the assistant news director, had asked Josh to contact us to investigate the building. We were joined by Gena Bilbo, the restaurant's marketing manager; Kelly Spurlock, a local psychic medium; and Angela Lynn, president/CEO of Sixth Sense World® Historic Ghost & Cemetery Tours.

When my wife and I arrived at the location, we all sat down with Gena to discuss the paranormal activity that was occurring in the restaurant. According to Gena, the majority of the staff feared the basement of the building the most. Even she refused to enter the basement area alone. In addition, the service staff regularly heard their names called out from right behind them, only to turn around and discover they were the only ones there. They also experienced the feeling of being watched by unseen eyes. "You never really feel alone in this building," remarked Gena.

THE HAUNTINGS

One of the more strange incidents occurred near the stairwell leading to the second floor. There is a huge alligator that hangs there which must weigh quite a few hundred pounds. One afternoon during service the alligator all of a sudden began to swing back and forth rapidly, as if it was a mere pendulum. Staff and patrons sat in awe while it continued to swing for a few more moments, then it suddenly stopped.

Although the restaurant had been experiencing strange activity since their recent occupation of the building the year before in 2012, it seemed that whatever entities were here dated to much earlier times. The building is just a stone's throw away from where a large slave market used to sit in what is now Ellis Square. The majority of the diners in the restaurant looking out of the second floor windows upon the square have no idea of the atrocities that occurred there during the years of slavery that still remain to be untold.

A GRAVE PAST

Slavery was a very common practice in the city of Savannah, not to mention the thousands of slaves that existed during the Antebellum period throughout the whole state of Georgia. According to Jeffrey Robert Young of Georgia State University in his

The B&D Burgers on Congress Street is nestled in one of
the most haunted sections of town.

article "Slavery in Antebellum Georgia," the number of slaves in the state were almost beyond comprehension. Young states that "In 1790, just before the explosion in cotton production, some 29,264 slaves resided in the state. By 1800, the slave population in Georgia had more than doubled to 59,699; by 1810, the number of slaves had grown to 105,218. In 1840, the slave population had increased to 280,944; and in 1860, on the eve of the Civil War (1861–1865), some 462,198 slaves constituted forty-four percent of the state's total population." Not to mention the majority of these slaves were first arriving in Savannah's ports to be sold at auction. Mothers and children, husbands and wives, all split up to be sold as property to the highest bidder.

THE HISTORY

The building at 209 West Congress Street now known as B&D Burgers was originally built in 1855, for Frederick Herb. Herb went on to own the property until it was later acquired by the Basch Brothers, who operated a clothing store there until the 1890s. It later went on to become a dry goods store, a pawn broker, and a wholesale clothing store. By 1913, a man by the name of J. J. Horrigan had opened a wholesale produce store in the building, and he continued to operate there until 1932.

After 1932, the Cobb Feed Company then acquired the building for a short while. In 1941, Samuel Bernstein opened a crockery and restaurant supply store on the property. He continued to thrive there until the 1980s, when it was converted into a print shop and postal store. By 2001, the property had become vacant and remained that way for many years. In November 2012, B&D Burgers Restaurant opened their second downtown Savannah location in this building.

THE INVESTIGATION

After getting all of the details from Gena about the strange activity in the building, I began setting up our cameras while Kim began going around getting base readings. As I was setting up one of the basement cameras my audio recorder happened to capture one of our first EVPs of the investigation. Upon playing my recorder back there was the voice of a small child who had clearly asked, "Hey, who is this?" This small spirit seemed to be curious as to what I was doing.

Almost as soon as she had started Kim was able to document very high levels of electromagnetic energy in the building, particularly in the basement, where most of the activity tends to occur. Even Kelly was picking up on a lot of readings in the basement. According to Kelly, there were definitely children spirits, as well as the spirits of slaves, both of whom had died in the building over the years. Even aside from Kim and Kelly's initial readings the basement had a very dismal, dense atmosphere.

CAUTION:
This building is
haunted.
We have an
agreement
with the
unseen to
only serve
USDA
CHOICE
ANGUS
BEEF
& they're
watching!

Evidently, the owners of B&D Burgers have an agreement
with the spirits over the quality of beef.

Once the investigation got underway we managed to capture a few other pieces of audio that were quite compelling. During an EVP session in the basement Kim asked, "Do you have children?" Right afterward a male spirit voice clearly replied with the answer, "Five." During that same EVP session Kim caught another piece of audio evidence when she asked, "Can you touch my hand?" and a spirit responded, "I shouldn't." We did have a few other interesting EVPs during the investigation, but the evidence that we captured in the basement was by far the most compelling. The investigation went on to air the following evening on WTGS-Fox News 28 and WJCL-ABC News in Savannah, and B&D Burgers on Congress Street still has reports of strange activity quite regularly.

If you happen to be near City Market in Savannah's Historic District pop in to B&D's for a burger and a beer; they have quite possibly the best burgers in all Savannah, not to mention a great craft beer list. Be sure to ask what the fry of the week is too, because they are constantly coming up with interesting new creations. I prefer the patio area, where they show all of the games on a huge projection screen, especially on Saturday and Sunday afternoons during football season. If you are lucky, you may even be able to talk one of the staff members into giving you a quick tour of the basement. If you do be sure to turn on an audio recorder, you may be surprised at what you may catch.

CHAPTER 6

REVENANTS AT THE ROUNDHOUSE

The Georgia State Railroad Museum Investigation

The Georgia State Railroad Museum sits over the site of one of the bloodiest battles of the American Revolution.

The site where the Georgia State Railroad Museum now sits is only a few feet away from where one of the most tragic events in Savannah's early history began. Although the railroad was built there in 1833, the property also contains the remnants of the Siege of Savannah Battlefield, where the second bloodiest battle of the Revolutionary War took place. The old railroad buildings and battlefield area have been riddled with ghosts for years, which considering the history of the place is not so surprising.

On the morning of December 29, 1778, British forces under the command of Lt. Col. Archibald Campbell marched into Savannah and captured the city. After a short skirmish with patriot forces Campbell had lost seven men in the battle, with another seventeen wounded. The colonists were not so lucky; their toll was eighty-three dead and eleven wounded, with 453 taken prisoner. It was not until almost a year later that Savannahians decided it was time to retake control of their city.

THE SIEGE OF SAVANNAH

In October 1779, American forces teamed up with the French, led by Comte d'Estaing, to attack a British fort on the west of the city. The French were accompanied by over 500 Haitian soldiers from Saint Domingue, including Henri Christophe, who later became president of Haiti. Just before dawn on the morning of October 9, 1779, the joint forces attacked the earthen British fort Spring Hill Redoubt on the west of town. The French were late to the attack and the dense fog disoriented the soldiers as they

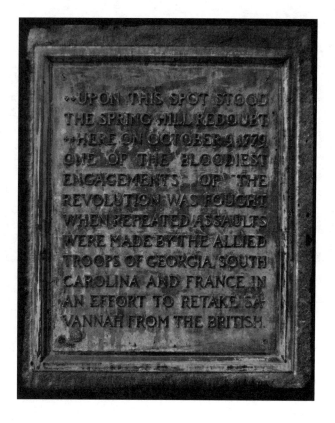

A historical marker designates the site where one of the bloodiest battles of the American Revolution took place.

approached the mound. The British soldiers, along with their Scottish Highlander allies, had no problem picking off the Franco-American forces as they advanced on the fort. Before long the trenches surrounding the redoubt began to fill with bodies. In less than an hour a truce was called to avoid further onslaught.

The British were victorious for a second time in Savannah, with their casualties totaling a mere fifty-five deaths, compared to the American allied forces who lost over 800 troops, over half of them being French. Among the dead were Sgt. William Jasper and Polish Count Casimir Pulaski, who aided the patriots in the attack. (Both now have monuments to their sacrifices: the Pulaski monument in Monterey Square and the Jasper monument in Madison Square.) With no time to dig individual graves before decomposition set in and disease became rampant, the corpses were buried in a mass grave just a short distance from where the battle occurred. A replica of the Spring Hill Redoubt now sits on Martin Luther King Boulevard not far from where the original stood. One officer who aided the Americans in the attack was Swedish Count Curt von Stedingk, who later wrote in his journal about the attack: "I had the pleasure of planting the American flag on the last trench, but the enemy renewed its attack and our people were annihilated by cross-fire. The moment of retreat with the cries of our dying comrades piercing my heart was the bitterest of my life."

A RAILROAD IS CONSTRUCTED

In December 1833, a charter was granted for the Central Railroad and Canal Company to build a railroad from Savannah to Macon, Georgia. The land they selected was right beside the old Siege of Savannah Battlefield. In 1835, the name was changed to the Central of Georgia Railroad and construction began. It was not until 1840 that the railroad saw its first full year of operation. William Washington Gordon was the founder and became the first president of the railroad. Gordon was mayor of Savannah from 1834 to 1836, and he was elected to the Georgia General Assembly in 1835, where he served as a member of the House of Representatives until later in 1838, when he was elected to the Georgia Senate. He was also the grandfather of Savannah's Juliette Gordon Low, founder of the Girl Scouts of America.

The railroad flourished for years, with 190 miles of track from Savannah to Macon transporting passengers and freight. By the 1850s, the complex consisted of a roundhouse, turntable, machine shop, blacksmith shop, and tender frame shop, as well as numerous other buildings. Most of these buildings have been preserved and are still viewable at the Georgia State Railroad Museum. Sadly, much of the railroad's success was due to cheap slave labor. Numerous deaths of these workers occurred due to the harsh conditions. Historian Theodore Kornweibel Jr. has found documented historical evidence that slaves were used on over seventy-five percent of the southern railroads. According to Kornweibel in *Railroads in the African American Experience*, over 10,000 slaves each year were railroad workers in the South between 1857 and 1865, and the Central of Georgia Railroad Company was no different.

A restored train engine sits in one of the
roundhouse bays of the old railroad museum.

DESECRATION OF THE MOUNDS

As if that was not bad enough, in 1843, the Central of Georgia Railroad destroyed a large portion of a Creek Indian Mound as they paved through it to extend their tracks. This mound, known as the Ocmulgee National Monument, was once again desecrated in 1873, when a second line was added. This time the line destroyed the funeral mound portion of the monument, where numerous bones were excavated as the track was placed. For a third time, on June 25, 1883, the railroad company again destroyed Indian burial ground when a monument was erected in the middle of Wright Square dedicated to William Washington Gordon, the railroad's founder. The only problem was the same spot was where Tomochichi, the Yamacraw Indian chief who aided Oglethorpe and the first settlers, was buried. Years later, on April 21, 1899, Gordon's daughter in-law, Nellie Kinzie Gordon, along with the Colonial Dames of America, had a new monument erected in the southeast of the square dedicated to the Indian chief.

During the Civil War much of the railroad was destroyed during Gen. William Sherman's infamous "March to the Sea." Much of the track was turned into "Sherman's neckties," where a portion of the track would be heated until it was pliable, then twisted to resemble a necktie. By 1866, under the direction of William Wadley, most of the railroad had been restored. The railroad continued to thrive up until the 1960s, when the structure was finally abandoned. In 1989, the Coastal Heritage Society acquired the property and they have owned it ever since. Before they acquired the place there were some small shops near the railroad complex. Around that area skulls with shocks of red hair attached to them were excavated. Believed to be the skulls of Scottish Highlanders who fought alongside the British in the Siege of Savannah, these skulls were put on display in the shop windows to attract curious customers. Soon after the skulls disintegrated as a result of exposure to the air.

The Coastal Heritage Society has now opened the complex to the public as the Georgia State Railroad Museum, complete with thirteen of the original buildings, a working turntable and roundhouse, and a children's museum. The property also contains the Savannah History Museum, which is in the railroad's old passenger depot, and the Siege of Savannah Battlefield. Since its reopening in 1989, there have been numerous reports of paranormal activity occurring throughout the grounds.

A WELL-DRESSED GHOST

Many people have reported seeing the apparition of a well-dressed gentleman standing on the end of the presidential railcar; he will appear for a few moments, then suddenly vanish into thin air. One afternoon, a small boy was visiting the museum with his mother when all of a sudden he stopped in his tracks and was frozen with shock. After calming down, he told his mother that he had just witnessed a tall gray man walk right through a brick wall near the old paint shop. The mother quickly gathered her child and after speaking to the staff about the incident, promptly left the museum.

It also seems the spirits that haunt the area are still trapped in the past. Employees have heard the phantom sounds of a printing press still running in the old print shop on numerous occasions, and many have heard footsteps creeping up behind them in the Tender Frame Shop when no one else was there. One of the most interesting occurrences deals with the computer system the museum uses. More than once an employee has come in to open up in the morning and all of the dates in the computer system had been set back to the 1850s. On a separate occasion, a CFO for the company went into the upstairs office and discovered a strange check on his desk. The check was numbered 1234567, and it was dated from the 1950s. He walked out of the room for a moment to ask a fellow employee if he had put it on his desk, and when he returned a few seconds later the check had disappeared. By meticulously preserving the past through renovating the railroad complex these spirits seem to continue on as if the railroad were still operating to this day.

In October 2013, I spoke to Frank Sulkowski, sports director and assistant news director for WJCL-ABC News and WTGS-FOX News 28 in Savannah. Our team had previously filmed four episodes of our show *Spooky Town* with him, and it was time to film a Halloween episode. A friend of mine in the Savannah Chamber of Commerce, Mindy Shea, suggested we investigate the Railroad Museum. She put me in touch with the director of the Coastal Heritage Society, a lady named Sandra Baxter, and we set a filming date of October 15. This was to be a three-part investigation, with full access to the whole railroad complex, the Siege of Savannah Battlefield, and the Savannah History Museum. In addition, we were also allowed access to the tunnels that ran underneath the museum.

THE INVESTIGATION

When we arrived that evening for the investigation the air was still and calm. We got started with our base readings just after midnight, and it was not long before we began to experience strange activity. Near the turntable an EVP was captured of an

Author Ryan Dunn and his wife Kim conduct an EVP session in an old railcar while filming an episode of their television series *Spooky Town*.

inquisitive spirit asking, "Who are you?" Evidently they were curious as to why we were there. More disturbing was when my wife Kim and I caught a chilling EVP in the railcar warehouse of a male entity that whispered, "They hurt me." Considering the harsh conditions that slaves endured while working there, this could have been one of them trying to communicate with us.

Throughout the night there was the overall feeling that we were not alone, and that whatever was with us was keeping a close watch on us. We did not catch anything unexplainable in the History Museum, but we did catch some rather compelling evidence on the old battlefield where the mass grave of soldiers was. A strange voice was recorded there of a male spirit clearly saying, "Bury it." With over 800 soldiers buried in a heap beneath the ground we stood on, it seemed obvious to what this entity was referring.

We investigated into the wee hours of the morning and finally decided to wrap things up just after 5 a.m. It was overall a very successful investigation and we were pleased to work with the Coastal Heritage Society for the first time. Their meticulous attention to preserving the past is an important asset to our great city. We went on to work with them again when we investigated Old Fort Jackson, which is mentioned later in this book. The museum is open seven days a week, and there is no better way to delve into Savannah's early past than to plan a visit here. You may even have a chance to encounter one of the many spirits that still haunt the grounds.

CHAPTER 7

SPIRITS & SHENANIGANS

The Kevin Barry's Irish Pub Investigation

Kevin Barry's Irish Pub is nestled in an old cotton warehouse along Savannah's riverfront.

In all of my years conducting paranormal research in Savannah, I am always drawn back to the River Street area to investigate. Once again, our team was granted overnight access to an old cotton warehouse along the riverfront, this time the haunted Kevin Barry's Irish Pub. Only a few buildings down from the old Chart House Restaurant we had investigated years before, I had been interested in investigating Kevin Barry's for quite a while. In spring 2014, I finally got my chance.

THE HISTORY

Kevin Barry's sits in an old cotton warehouse constructed in 1809 for Benjamin Burroughs, who leased the lot from Sarah Jones, the recently widowed wife of Savannah's infamous Noble Wimberly Jones. Not long after being built the warehouse was destroyed by fire in 1827. It was rebuilt, and an addition was added in 1854. In the early 1900s, it served as Kavanaugh & Company, a fruits and produce company. By the 1940s, it was converted into a warehouse for the Peters Bottling Company, then the structure remained vacant for numerous years. In 1981, Kevin Barry's Irish Pub was opened, which remains one of the best riverfront pubs to this day.

The restaurant was named after Irish hero Kevin Barry, who was a member of the IRA (Irish Republican Army) and fought against the British for Irish independence. In November 1920, Barry was executed at age eighteen for a raid on British trucks that resulted in the deaths of three British soldiers. Although Barry never fired a shot he refused to give up the names of his comrades, who had fled and left him to take the fall. To this day the restaurant honors the bravery of those who have fought for independence. On the second floor of the restaurant is Hero's Hall, which honors all of those who have served in any branch of the United States military. Hundreds of pictures line the walls of this room as a testament to those who gave their lives for our freedom. The photos of countless soldiers that lost their lives fill the room, still adorned with the lipstick imprints of loved ones' last kisses. It is impossible to enter this room and not feel any emotion as you look at the price of our freedom.

As with the majority of the properties along River Street, many of the hauntings in the building can be attributed to slavery. The old cotton warehouses that line River

Street have now been converted into a myriad of restaurants, bars, and gift shops, but the original uses for these buildings paint a much darker picture. Although slavery was originally illegal in the colony of Georgia, by 1750, there was a repeal on the ban of slaves. Men, women, and even young children were forced to spend the rest of their lives working without end, and the cotton warehouses along Savannah's docks proved to be some of the harshest conditions. Slaves were forced to work all day on the docks, then slept in cramped warehouses with very little to keep them warm. Many died due to illness, disease, and exposure to the elements. Echoes of these tragedies still reverberate throughout these old buildings, and Kevin Barry's Irish Pub is no different.

Three days after Savannah's infamous Saint Patrick's Day festival I had a meeting with Tara Reese, the manager and events coordinator for Kevin Barry's, which seemed only fitting, considering the fact we were dealing with an Irish pub. Savannah has the second largest Saint Patrick's Day celebration in the United States, so waiting until at least three days after the festivities was almost a necessity. As Tara began to describe the paranormal events that occurred there on a regular basis I began to grin from ear to ear, knowing we had just landed a great location. Aside from lights turning themselves on and off and the occasional phantom footsteps coming from the upper floors there were a lot of other occurrences that were even more unsettling.

THE INCIDENT WITH THE LAMP

One afternoon, Tara was walking down the staircase leading to the first floor of the building. There is an old desk lamp with a clip clamped to the wall near the bottom of the stairs. As Tara walked past, the lamp suddenly went flying through the air and landed about thirty feet away. As she turned around no one was standing near the lamp, and all of the customers at the bar were shocked with disbelief. Not only would it have taken tremendous energy for an entity to throw a lamp across the room, but the lamp was plugged into the wall, which meant it took quite a bit of force to jerk it from its socket and land some thirty feet away. Tara, who is somewhat of a skeptic, had no explanation for what had just happened.

On another occasion, Tara arrived at work early one morning at around 8:00 a.m. She was the only one in the building and she had just walked into the kitchen, which was pitch dark. As she entered the room she heard a clear female voice say, "Good morning." Realizing she was not as alone as she thought Tara quickly left the kitchen. This female presence has also been witnessed by one of the pub's regular customers, who wishes to remain unnamed. He reported to Tara one afternoon that he had just seen an apparition of a young female in a long white dress standing on the stairs. He said the woman stood there for a few moments and then just vanished into thin air.

The front door to Kevin Barry's Irish Pub is adorned with stickers from various military branches and divisions in support of our troops.

One early morning around 5:00 a.m., Jim, the building's maintenance man, had his own personal paranormal experience. Not long after he arrived he heard the distinct sound of a man coughing. The sound was coming from the back of the restaurant, near where the restrooms are on the first floor. He was alone in the building, but he went to check where the sound was coming from and discovered the restaurant empty. He returned to his work, but shortly afterward he heard the coughing sound yet again, this time louder. Since this occurrence Jim does not like being alone in the building, and quite understandably so.

THROWING BRICKS

The music room on the main floor tends to be one of the most active rooms in the building; guests are able to enjoy traditional Irish fare while listening to live Irish music seven nights a week. One customer named Gary Bryant, known to his friends as "Fuzz," had his own paranormal experience in this room. Fuzz, a retired military veteran, and his wife visit Savannah at least once a year to celebrate their anniversary, and the trip is never complete without a visit to their favorite restaurant, Kevin Barry's Irish Pub.

One evening a few years back they were having dinner in the music room while enjoying the Celtic music being performed on stage. It was a peculiarly slow night at the restaurant and they were the only ones in the dining room. All of a sudden Fuzz heard a loud thud on the floor next to he and his wife. At first he ignored the sound, but then it kept occurring. Annoyed with the incessant noise, he looked on the ground beside him and noticed a small pile of bricks sitting there on the floor. He quickly glanced around the room and realized that they were still the only ones there save for the musician on the stage. It was as if some angered spirit was tossing bricks at them. The next question in my mind was where did the bricks come from?

In April 2014, we had our chance to meet the entities that haunt Kevin Barry's head on. My wife Kim and I arrived at the pub just after 2 a.m. as they were closing to begin setting up for that night's investigation. As we were still unpacking one of our audio recorders caught a recording of a female voice that whispered, "Ryan." It seemed that these entities knew who we were as soon as we arrived. As the night went on the more active the spirits became.

THE DEVIL'S TOY BOX

We had brought with us a new piece of equipment known as the "Devil's Toy Box" to experiment with on the investigation. It is not nearly as wicked as the name suggests, and actually has nothing to do with the Devil. This is a piece of equipment developed by engineer Bill Chappell, who owns Digital Dowsing. Bill and his equipment have appeared on the *Ghost Adventures* television show many times, and he has developed some of the most important equipment that we use in the field to this day. This particular piece of equipment consists of a six-sided mirror box with a hinged lid in which a piezoelectric microphone is attached. Spirits are said to be attracted to mirrors, and the theory is that this box can temporarily trap entities and capture them on recording. The majority of the equipment that we use during our paranormal investigations is purely scientific, but we are always willing to try new things to get even more results.

Later in the evening we had wired an audio recorder to the Devil's Toy Box during an EVP session in the downstairs dining room. Not long after we began asking questions the hinge of the box flapped closed by itself and the recorder caught the sound of something bouncing around inside it. This in turn caused the box to skip a few inches across the table where it had been placed. We were sitting about fifteen feet away from the box when the incident occurred and were completely floored by what had just happened. We were not able to find a rational explanation for what we had just witnessed.

AN ANGRY SPIRIT

One of the best audio recordings came later in the evening, and it was none too happy with me. Around 4:00 a.m., while conducting an EVP session in the downstairs dining room with Kim and Tara, my audio recorder caught the voice of an angry male spirit that growled, "Hurt him." I was the only male on the investigation that evening, so I assumed this comment was directed toward me. Not twenty seconds after this strange recording was captured a loud crash came from the corner of the room, as if someone had just thrown a bunch of metal pots at the ballast stone wall of the restaurant. The loud noise reverberated throughout the entire building, startling all three investigators. After looking near where the sound had initially occurred there was nothing out of place, nor anything to account for the strange noise.

Overall, the investigation proved to be a success. We walked away with some great evidence and quite a few documented personal experiences. We were able to document multiple entities in the building, male and female. These spirits seem to coexist with the living here, but occasionally they tend to make themselves known.

Whenever visiting Kevin Barry's Irish Pub do not forget to try a cup of their traditional Irish soup, which is perfect on those rainy days while strolling along the riverfront. Before you leave don't forget to visit Hero's Hall and pay respects to all of those who have dedicated their very lives for our freedom.

THE PRIVATE GARRITY INCIDENT

The Old Fort Jackson Investigation

Fort Jackson sits along the Savannah River just to the east of the historic district.

Just to the east of Savannah's Historic District, along the Savannah River, sits historic Old Fort Jackson. Strangely enough, although the fort never saw battle, many deaths still occurred there due to the harsh living conditions. Ghosts of the past still resonate within the fort's walls, and many a visitor and employee have reported paranormal occurrences there for years. The dark history of the land before the fort was even built could account for some of the hauntings, but reports of phantom soldiers also happen quite often.

SALTER'S ISLAND

Before Savannah's first settlers arrived in 1733, the land where the colony of Savannah was established (and its surrounding areas) was inhabited by the Yamacraw Indians. Less than 1,600 yards from where present day Fort Jackson sits a set of Indian ceremonial mounds rests, still showing signs of our area's earliest history. Not long after the first settlers arrived a brick mason named Thomas Salter started making bricks where Fort Jackson now sits. The small island was later named "Salter's Island" after Thomas Salter. After later moving his business to Hutchinson Island, a mud fort was built on the island in 1778. Being along the swampy area of the river, the fort was rampant with mosquitoes. Soon after the fort was built, in February of that year Capt. Thomas Lee and nearly three-quarters of his one hundred troops stationed there had died of malaria and other mosquito-related diseases.

During the American Revolution warships were docked at Five Fathom Hole near the mud fort in 1779, but it was not until 1808 that the current fort was built. The fort was built after a letter was sent to President Thomas Jefferson suggesting that Savannah needed defenses along its river front. The fort was named after James Jackson, United States Senator, Georgia governor, and Revolutionary War hero. To this day Fort Jackson is one of only eight forts in the United States still standing that was built prior to the War of 1812. Throughout the 1800s, soldiers were stationed at the fort periodically, while other years it remained abandoned. By 1861, it was reported that Fort Jackson had "one 32 pounder rifled navy gun, five 32 pounder navy guns, and three 18 pounders." (OR Series 1, Volume 6, Chapter 15. *Correspondence, orders, and returns relating to operations on the coast of South Carolina, Georgia, and middle and East Florida from August 21, 1861, to April 11, 1862*. Savannah, GA, November 27, 1861, Capt. T. A. Washington to Assistant Adjutant General)

PRIVATE GARRITY

On the evening of June 12, 1862, a strange incident happened at the fort. Two companies were stationed there at the time: the Republican Blues and the Emmett Rifles. Author Roger S. Durham recounts the incident in full detail in *The Blues in Gray: The Civil War Journal of William Daniel Dixon and the Republican Blues Daybook*. Lt. George W. Dickerson of the Republican Blues was approached by Pvt. Patrick Garrity of the Emmett Rifles. Garrity fired his weapon at Dickerson, but the gun did not go off. He then clubbed Dickerson over the head with the gun, then continued to deliver blow after blow to Dickerson's head and shoulders with the butt of the gun. Garrity then jumped over the moat of the fort and drowned in the thickening mud; his corpse was pulled out of the muck the very next day. Dickerson recovered over time, but never fully, as he remained permanently disfigured for the rest of his life. Garrity had seemed completely normal prior to the incident and the listed cause for the attack was insanity.

THE FORT IS DESERTED

In December 1864, the night before Gen. William Sherman arrived with his Union troops, the Confederate soldiers rallied at Fort Jackson before they escaped later that night to Hardeeville, South Carolina. Throughout the late 1800s and early 1900s, the fort fell into disrepair. In 1958, the fort was turned over to the state of Georgia, but it was not until early 1976 that the Coastal Heritage Society took over and reopened the place to the public on Labor Day weekend of that year. The Coastal Heritage Society continues to maintain the property with attention to detail and historical accuracy, complete with daily cannon firings.

The drawbridge where Pvt. Patrick Garraty jumped to his death shortly after bludgeoning Lt. Dickerson almost to death.

Considering we had investigated the other three properties owned by the Coastal Heritage Society (The Georgia State Railroad Museum, the Siege of Savannah Battlefield, and the Visitor's Center Museum on MLK Boulevard—previously part of the old railroad station), it seemed only fitting that we also investigate Old Fort Jackson. With all of the history and hauntings surrounding the area, I spoke with their director and set up an investigation for June 19, 2014.

A few weeks prior to the investigation my photographer, Ryan Reese, and I met with Ray Christy, one of the employees of the fort and one of the most knowledgeable people I have ever met. We spoke at great lengths about everything he had experienced while working there. According to Ray, many visitors have reported seeing the apparition of a Confederate soldier standing near the drawbridge of the fort who is believed to be the ghost of Pvt. Patrick Garraty.

One evening, during a private party held at the fort, Ray and a few others were working the function dressed fully in period soldiers' outfits. Several guests had approached Ray and the other employees throughout the night inquiring as to whom the small boy was they kept seeing running around during the party. It being an all adult party, they found it strange that there was a small child running around on the loose. Ray and the other employees then assured the guests that there were no children at the party. Later that evening, after all of the guests had left and the staff was cleaning up, one employee witnessed the apparition of a small boy in a long white night shirt run past the great gates of the fort and disappear. This was a strange occurrence because there are no reports of children ever living in the fort. Could this possibly have been one of Thomas Salter's children who died here many years before when his family made bricks where the fort now sits?

A few months later Ray witnessed his own apparition at the fort. He was finishing up his workday one sunny afternoon, and he had just closed and locked all the doors. Out of the corner of his eye he suddenly saw the apparition of a Confederate soldier in a gray uniform walk into the fort. This would have been impossible, because the entity would have had to walk directly through the fort's wall to gain entry, since all of the doors and gates had been locked just a few minutes before. After a few moments the apparition disappeared and Ray quickly finished up his work and left.

A SILENT SOLDIER

Neil Moore, another employee and fort guide, had quite a few interesting stories to share as well. One afternoon, a man came up to Neil extremely upset and said: "You need to do something about that guy in the guard room." Neil, who was concerned that maybe another visitor was being disruptive, asked the man, "What's going on?" The angry man then replied: "Well, there is a man dressed as a soldier in the guard room. I have asked him several questions and he never responded or even bothered to

The interior of Fort Jackson, home to numerous ghosts.

turn around and address me." Neil looked at the man and said truthfully, "Sir, I'm the only employee dressed as a soldier in the fort today." All of the color left the man's face and he then left the fort rather quickly.

Another incident occurred at the fort late one night after a private event. Everyone had been gone for hours, with the exception of two employees who were still in the fort. One of them was standing in the middle of the fort smoking a cigarette when he suddenly saw a male soldier in a blue uniform walk out of the jail cell and enter the guard room. Convinced it was his fellow employee, who also happened to be wearing a blue uniform that night, he shouted: "Come on out of the guard room so we can finish closing up!" All of a sudden from behind him he heard his coworker shout, "Hey man, I'm over here!" The man then said: "Well, there's a man in a blue uniform standing in the guard room, I'm outta here!"

THE INVESTIGATION

According to Ray and Neil, there were more than enough stories surrounding the old structure to warrant an investigation. I arrived at the fort on June 19, 2014, with my photographer, Ryan Reese. The sun had just fallen behind the horizon, and the fort had an ominous glow as we slowly drove down the road. After again speaking briefly with Neil and Ray we began to set up our equipment. It had been a while since I had conducted an investigation with only one other investigator, but tonight Ryan and I were excited to have the place to ourselves. After getting initial base readings we grabbed our walkie talkies and then split up.

Not long after we had split up I was conducting an EVP session in the powder magazine of the fort. Save for the soft glow of the moonlight lighting the doorway I was in complete darkness. Within minutes I witnessed a three-dimensional, tall dark shadow enter the doorway and block out part of the light, silhouetting its shadowy form in greater detail. At first I thought my eyes were playing tricks on me, or that Reese had come down from the battlements where he had been taking long exposure shots. I radioed Reese, who responded he had not left his position. I looked at the doorway and this being was walking slowly toward where I was sitting! It came within two to three feet of where I was standing, then vaporized. All of a sudden the room was freezing cold and my Mel meter documented a fifteen degree temperature drop.

Later in that same room, during an EVP session that I conducted with Ryan Reese, he asked: "Who is the child that runs by at night?" Our audio recorder then captured a small voice that replied, "It is I." We believe this may be the same child that has been witnessed haunting the fort before. One of the most compelling EVPs was captured near the cannon at the top of the fort, which was actually used in the Battle of New Orleans. While recording I asked: "Whose side are you on?" A very clear male voice then replied, "South." It seemed obvious as to where the allegiance of this fort's spirits lay. Later that night, while walking down the drawbridge of the fort, I asked: "Where are you, is there anyone here?" On the playback my recorder captured a Class A EVP of a male entity that clearly replied, "Go right." This may have been the ghost of Pvt. Patrick Garrity leading us to where he had jumped to a watery grave many years before.

The jail cell of the fort also tended to be highly active. At one point during the investigation I had been sitting in the jail cell doing an EVP session by myself when I heard Ryan Reese shouting "Where are you?" a few rooms away. I replied, "I'm over here." On the playback my audio recorder then caught the voice of an angry male spirit who growled, "Quiet." It seems the spirits in the fort do not enjoy loud voices. Late into the night, as we were wrapping up the investigation, in the jail cell I asked: "If you want us to leave then please give us a sign." A few seconds later an EVP was caught of a male clearly saying, "We want you to leave." Clearly

The building that used to house the Tybee Island Railroad Depot is now used as the gift shop and front office for Fort Jackson.

we had overstayed our welcome. We then started to wrap things up and let the spirits return to their rest.

Having the unique opportunity to investigate this amazing historic location yielded some great results. I have always enjoyed investigating forts; there is something surreal and almost magical about being there after closing, all alone in the old structures. You get a feel for what it might have been like to have been stationed there so many years ago. It seems although the fort did not experience any battles, there have been plenty of deaths associated with the property which could explain why there are so many here that are still in a state of unrest. If you ever get the opportunity I highly recommend a visit to Old Fort Jackson, it is well worth the trip. It is rare that you find a piece of history like this that has been so well preserved. Be aware of your surroundings, though, because what might at first glance seem like a fort employee in uniform may very well be a ghost.

CHAPTER 9

Caution: Children at Play

The Hamilton-Turner Inn Investigation

The Hamilton-Turner Inn, home to the restless spirits of playful children.

On the east end of Lafayette Square, just about a block away from the Cathedral of St. John the Baptist, sits the Hamilton-Turner Inn. An excellent example of southern charm at its finest, this mansion stands as a testament to the opulence that Savannah's early elite relished in. The home is now a luxurious bed and breakfast that boasts more accolades than any other stay in the city, including being listed as one of America's Most Romantic Hotels by *Travel + Leisure*. Among being one of the most lavish hotels in the city it has also been listed as one of the most haunted.

THE HISTORY

The home sits on a lot purchased from Gilbert Butler by Mr. Samuel Pugh Hamilton. Mr. Hamilton and his second wife (his deceased brother's widow), Sarah Virginia Hamilton, built this beautiful southern mansion in 1873. To say that the Hamiltons were of the upper crust of Savannah would be an understatement. Mr. Hamilton was a jeweler, president of the Brush Electric and Power Company, and president of Merchants National Bank, in addition to being a devout member of the Masons. Being that Mr. Hamilton was president of the power company, his house was the very first home in Savannah to have electricity. In 1886, the home boasted electric lights throughout the entire house, which the neighbors then feared would cause the home to explode.

According to the 1880 census, the Hamiltons had six children ranging from five to twenty-two years of age. Two of these children were from Mrs. Hamilton's first marriage to Samuel's brother. The Hamiltons continued to live in splendor for many years until tragedy struck in 1898. By summer of that year Mr. Hamilton's twenty-three-year-old daughter, Virginia Lee Hamilton, was diagnosed with what was then known as "chlorosis," more commonly called the "green sickness." This disease in those days was considered a mental sickness, where the afflicted would have loss of appetite, weight loss, and severe headaches, and it could result in death. The disease gets its name by the green color it caused of the patient's skin. This is now known to be hypochromic anemia—a disease caused by vitamin B6 deficiency and low iron intake—which could have been caused by a multitude of reasons, including infections caused by hookworms, lead poisoning, or other such disease.

After watching their young daughter slowly wither away, on August 6, 1898, Virginia Lee Hamilton finally succumbed to the disease. According to her obituary, the funeral was held in the front parlor of the Hamilton home, and as it states, "the deep affection in which Miss Hamilton was held by her acquaintances, and her sudden taking away, made the service one of the keenest sorrow." Less than a year later Mr. Hamilton died in the home on June 22, 1899, of heart failure at age sixty-two. His wife, Sarah, joined him on January 11, 1920, when she died from obstructive jaundice, a condition caused by the blockage of the flow of bile from the liver.

In 1922, the home was sold to Mr. Francis M. Turner and his wife Bonnie. There have been many rumors that Mr. Turner was a physician who performed abortions at his office in the home, yet these have been proven to be untrue. Mr. Turner was in fact a doctor, yet he was an osteopathic physician, not an abortion doctor, and his office was actually at 24 West Jones Street, not in his home. For a few years the home was used to house the nurses of the nearby Marine Hospital, then the Turners moved back to the home in 1937. The Turners continued to live in the house with their daughters, Mary and Winifred Turner, until Francis succumbed to what was deemed a coronary insufficiency in 1961. Mrs. Turner continued to live in the home for a few more years as a widow until she moved to Atlanta, Georgia, and the home became vacant in 1966.

JOE ODOM'S HOUSE MUSEUM

The mansion remained vacant until 1978, when it was split up into separate apartments. Throughout the late 1980s and early 1990s, Nancy Hillis, known for her character in John Berendt's best-selling novel *Midnight in the Garden of Good and Evil*, owned the home as separate apartments and a house museum. Another of the book's more colorful characters, Joe Odom, lived in the house during this time as well. This is also the home mentioned in the book in which Joe Odom would have all of the tour buses stop by to unload tourists, who would then pay admission to the "house museum" that he ran there. This was just one of the many money-making schemes concocted by Odom mentioned in Berendt's book. In 1997, Charlie and Sue Strickland remodeled the entire mansion and converted it into one of Savannah's most successful B&Bs, the Hamilton-Turner Inn. The inn is now run by Innkeeper Susie Ridder, who continues to operate one of the most luxurious stays in all of Savannah.

THE HAUNTINGS

Susie has a few interesting stories to share concerning the inn's hauntings. One morning, Susie received a complaint from a young couple who were staying in room 105. They were upset about how they had laid in bed all night hearing loud, raucous laughter and partying going on in the main parlor above them all night. Susie politely explained to the couple that there had been no such event going on the night before, and she was not able to find a cause for the loud noises they had heard. Although Susie has had a few strange experiences in the home, it was Tim O'Beirne, the inn's concierge, who had quite a few exciting incidents to share with me. As the two of us sat in the parlor of the inn one sunny July morning discussing the hauntings in the old home my heart began to speed up with anticipation of the upcoming investigation.

One of Tim's most memorable experiences had happened a few months before while he was in the carriage house. One morning Tim had entered the carriage house, and he distinctly remembered closing the gate behind him as he went. While he was on the second floor he heard a loud female voice downstairs that seemed to be calling his name. As he walked down the stairs the door to the carriage house was wide open, and so was the gate that led to the main house. On top of that, to his astonishment, there was no one to be seen that could have spoken or opened the gate and the door. According to Tim, the majority of the housekeepers will not even go into the carriage house because they swear it is haunted. In another incident Tim was in room 201 one morning, and he had opened the armoire where an ironing board and iron sat. Upon exiting the room Tim heard a loud thud from behind him. When he turned around and reentered the room the ironing board and iron that had been in the closet only moments before were now set up and sitting in the middle of the floor of the room.

Many guests staying at the inn regularly report inexplicable encounters with the ghosts that haunt the place. On one occasion, a lady staying in room 202 was awakened around 12:30–1:00 a.m. to what sounded like furniture being moved around in the room above her (room 302). She was all upset at breakfast the following morning, complaining about the noises that were coming from the room above her the night before. The guests who were staying in room 302 happened to be seated at the table next to her. They explained to the lady: "Well, we are staying in that very room, but we didn't return last night until well after 2:00 a.m., so the noises that you heard could not have been us." Still others have regularly reported seeing a man in period dress standing at the bottom of the staircase that leads from the first to the second floor. It is believed this is the ghost of Mr. Hamilton, still watching over his home after all these years.

⇒ A NOISY SPIRIT

One woman who was staying on the third floor had an experience so unnerving that she told Tim the following morning about her strange encounter the night before. She went on to explain that while she was trying to fall asleep she felt like something kept touching her while she was lying in bed. Right after the strange touching sensation started her closet doors began to open and close by themselves. This happened twice before it suddenly stopped. According to Tim the inn has heavy, old historic doors which do not easily open and close, especially on their own.

Another common occurrence reported by guests at the inn involves the sounds of children running down the halls. As a rule, the Hamilton-Turner Inn does not allow children to stay there, yet guests still frequently complain about hearing children's laughter in the halls late at night, in addition to the sounds of children playing. When they explain to the staff what they heard they are always told the same thing: there are no children staying at the inn.

In addition to the occurrences described by Tim, I have heard strange stories from guests taking my ghost tour about their own experiences while staying there. A couple that took my tour had a strange experience one night in room 402. While on my tour I had explained to them how you could use a smart phone's voice recording app to capture EVPs. They decided to turn theirs on to record and had set it on the nightstand while they slept. The following morning, as they listened to the recording, they were astonished at what they had captured. Late into the night, all of a sudden there was the sound of a jack-in-the-box slowly cranking. As the sound of the music became louder and louder there was the sudden sound of it popping out of the box. Right afterward an unexplainable male voice whispered, "Sshhh, it's almost morning."

THE INVESTIGATION

When we arrived for the investigation that night the feeling was bittersweet. This was to be our photographer Ryan Reese's last investigation with the team. Ryan had put in years of hard work with the team and it was hard to see such a great asset leave us, but he left under good circumstances. It was just his time to move on from the paranormal research field and on to other forms of photography. At the same time this was to be Kris Kersten's first official investigation with the team as an investigator in training. Kris had been on a few other cases with us, but now we had decided to bring him into the fold. Now our equipment technician and photographer, Kris has since gone on to be my right-hand man and an excellent paranormal investigator.

We had arrived for the investigation just after 8:00 p.m., but it was not until almost 10 p.m. that we captured our first EVP. The three of us had split up and were all in separate rooms of the inn conducting EVP sessions. While I was in room 501 my audio recorder caught the clear voice of an intelligent male spirit that said, "We want no trouble." It seemed the spirits haunting the inn were concerned about our presence there, but it did not take long before they began communicating more openly. Around 10:30 p.m., I was conducting an EVP session in room 304 and my audio recorder captured the clear recording of a little girl that asked, "Can you help me?" My first reaction to hearing this chilling EVP was that this may indeed be one of the spirits of the children that inn guests have reported hearing quite regularly.

Although we were catching some compelling audio evidence early on, it was just before midnight when we managed to capture something that may have tied directly to the history of the home. As the three of us were conducting an EVP session in room 201 an audio recorder that had been placed in the middle of the room captured two EVPs less than fifteen seconds apart. The first one was the voice of a male spirit that distinctly whispered, "Headache." A few seconds later the same voice whispered, "Get help." Could this have possibly been the room in which Virginia Lee Hamilton died during summer 1898? We just may have caught the voice of Mr. Hamilton calling for help for his dying young daughter. Also, the fact that severe headaches were a common symptom of chlorosis means he quite possibly could have been describing his daughter's symptoms just before he called for help.

Throughout the entire night the whole team experienced strange feelings, especially in rooms 104, 201, 202, 304, and 501. It was almost as if some unseen presence were standing just beyond sight, watching us anxiously as we conducted our research. We caught a few other pieces of audio throughout the night, but nothing that was malevolent in nature. There were definitely spirits haunting the inn, but most seemed to be at peace, and the others, if anything, actually seemed to be lost.

If you are looking for a luxurious stay in our beautiful hostess city I highly recommend the Hamilton-Turner Inn. You can lavish in the opulence once enjoyed by the Hamilton and Turner families, as well as get a feel for the aristocratic side of Savannah's earlier years. While you are there be sure to ask Susie and Tim about the latest ghost stories experienced by the inn's guests. With the inn being as active as it is there are new stories almost every other day. If you are staying in room 402 make sure you leave a recorder rolling while you sleep; you may be able to catch the recording of the child playing with the jack-in-the-box. If you do decide to try and record EVPs during your stay I do not recommend you go back and listen to any of the recordings until you return home from your trip. If you do you very well may not stay another night in Savannah.

CHAPTER 10

BOOS, BREWS & BOURBON

The Congress Street Social Club
Investigation

Many buildings along Congress Street were originally used as storage warehouses for slaves who were sold at auction just around the corner in the Slave Market. The Congress Street Social Club is no different.

It was in my friend James Caskey's 2012 edition of *Haunted Savannah* that I first learned about the hauntings at the Congress Street Social Club. Prior to being the Social Club, which opened in 2011, B&B Billiards occupied this building. According to Caskey, the owners of B&B had been dealing with paranormal activity there for quite a few years.

THE HISTORY

The building that now houses the Congress Street Social Club sits at 411 West Congress Street, and was constructed in 1860. The structure was the home of J. M. Denmark & Company, a grocery and liquor store throughout its earliest years. It later housed a flour and feed company, then became the home of Daniel G. Heidt in the 1890s. Heidt operated a wagon yard and boarding stable there, as well as resided in the building. Throughout the early 1900s it was home to a shoe store, a harness maker, and a furniture business. It then went on to become the International Harvester Company, the Indian Motorcycle Company, and later a drug store. The building remained vacant for many years throughout the 1970s and '80s, then it was opened as B&D Billiards in the 1990s. When the Social Club arrived in 2011, they began to experience strange occurrences almost immediately.

I met Tim Gardiner one spring afternoon in 2014 to discuss the paranormal events that were happening at his restaurant. According to Tim, many staff members over the years have reported hearing the sounds of pots and pans clanking around in the kitchen late at night after closing. Others have heard strange footsteps walking around the restaurant when no one else is there. It seems a lot of the activity occurs in the women's restroom on the main floor. The stall doors there tend to open and slam shut by themselves. One manager named Art had a strange experience one afternoon when he went to clean the restroom. As he was starting to clean, the toilet paper on one of the holders began to unspool itself at an alarming rate! It was as if something or someone was rolling it out, yet Art was the only one in the room.

I asked Tim if he had ever experienced anything strange since he started working there. "The strangest thing that I have ever witnessed here was electrical related," stated Tim. "I know that we are in an old building and it isn't uncommon to have electrical surges from time to time, but this was different. One evening two of our televisions, our bar rope lights, and our patio lights simultaneously went out. There are two different circuits running all of these, but of course I suspected a power surge. As I went to check it out I noticed the plugs that run both the power strips had been physically removed from their sockets."

THE TALL MAN

As we were finishing up the interview Tim had one more thing to add, and this seemed to be the most unnerving. "I have heard for years that many people have seen a strange tall man in a wide-brimmed hat sitting at the end of the bar in the basement," said Tim. "When the bartenders approach him to ask what he would like to drink the man simply vanishes." After wrapping up the interview we set a date of mid-August for the investigation.

INVESTIGATION

When I arrived at the Congress Street Social Club just after 2 a.m. for the investigation there was a strange feeling in the air. I had been interested in investigating there for years, but this was our first investigation without our photographer, Ryan Reese. Reese had been with our team since early 2011, and he had just recently left to pursue other interests. We parted ways amicably and still remain good friends, but it still felt strange not having him along. I was very excited to have Kris Kersten, our equipment tech, along with me, who had just recently joined our team. He has since been a great addition, and adding him to our group remains one of the best decisions that my wife Kim and I have ever made.

The Congress Street Social Club has experienced paranormal activity ever since they opened.

As is our protocol, we always conduct a series of base readings as we begin every single investigation. We look for readings in temperature, humidity, and EMF (electromagnetic fields), and that way if we find any anomalies during the investigation we have something to base them against. As I was walking down the back stairway I was able to get an extremely high EMF spike near the wall. Although EMF detectors are used to detect the presence of a ghost, they can also detect electromagnetic fields caused by power boxes, electrical circuitry, and other such devices. I discovered the power box behind the wall was the reason for this high reading, but spirits are attracted to this energy, and with the high levels of EMF in the building this place was possibly, as they say in the classic movie *Ghostbusters*, "Spook Central."

Later into the night Kris and I were conducting an EVP session in the women's restroom, since that tended to be one of the most active spots in the building. As soon as we entered the room the air was thick and dense. There was a heavy presence there, and we knew right away that we were not alone. Soon after we began we caught a recording of a strange moaning sound that appeared to be the voice of a female. It sounded as if this woman was in great pain. We were the only ones in the room, or so we thought, so there was no rational explanation for the strange sound. A few minutes later Kris asked: "Why are you still here? Are you trapped here?" A moment later one of our audio recorders captured the voice of a male entity that replied, "I need help." We managed to capture a few other strange things throughout the evening, but this one was the most chilling.

We did not catch a ton of evidence during our investigation, but we were able to walk away with a few Class A EVPs from throughout the night. We were definitely able to determine the place to be haunted by more than one entity, and these spirits seemed quite restless, to say the least. The Social Club is one of the best places in town to grab a bite and watch a game, not to mention they have the most extensive list of rare small-batch bourbons in town, with over one hundred to choose from; the patio is always packed during the summer. If you decide to sit at the bar keep an eye out for the tall man in the wide-brimmed hat. Perhaps this time he may actually stay for a drink.

CHAPTER 11

ROCKET MAN

The 315 West Bolton Street Investigation

The female spirit haunting 315 West Bolton Street has been witnessed by numerous people over the years.

avannah, although world renowned for its haunts, also bolsters a wide array of colorful characters that make up our unique city. John Berendt's bestselling novel *Midnight in the Garden of Good and Evil* portrays many of these interesting individuals with the backdrop of Savannah's elegant charm. When my wife and I arrived in town in 2010 to begin a new chapter in our lives, we moved in next door to one of the most interesting people that I have ever met, named Jim Hendricksen. He is known to many simply as "Crazy Jim." Jim earned his nickname due to his no-holds-barred, fly-by-the-seat-of-his-pants attitude and his eagerness to blow stuff up.

Jim is a very interesting neighbor indeed, as he spends much of his spare time launching rockets. By rockets I do not mean the kind you may purchase at Walmart or other such stores. The kind of rockets Jim is involved with have to be launched in the desert, and he has special clearance to fire off some of the largest rockets available. He has launched everything from coffins to television sets attached to these things. You may have even seen him on the Science Channel's program entitled *Large Dangerous Rocket Ships*, hosted by Kari Byron from the hit television show *Mythbusters*. Jim has appeared on the show numerous times, launching rockets and blowing stuff up. Not only does he launch these rockets, but he has written many manuals on how to build them; he is very well known in the world of rocketry, to say the least. My wife and I have spent many a night in our courtyard having cocktails and watching Jim light discs of pure rocket fuel on fire just for fun.

Although we live in Savannah's Historic District, which is one of the most beautiful areas in the Southeast to live, in the 1980s, downtown was a dangerous place to live. Many of the beautiful Victorian mansions were in much need of repair, and the area was not nearly as safe as it is now. After years of extensive renovations and a great police force the city has cleaned it up and we now take great pride in our city. When Jim moved into 315 West Bolton Street he encountered quite a few problems with crime in the neighborhood. According to Jim there used to be a pay phone at the end of the street. Drug dealers with pagers would hang around the pay phone late at night, making suspicious deals, and prostitutes would wait on the corners for passersby. Jim would repeatedly call the police, who would patrol the area, but as soon as they left the riffraff would return.

SHOOTING HOOKERS

"I finally decided that it was time to take matters into my own hands," Jim told us one evening. "I went out to Kmart and bought an air rifle. I went up to the second floor of my house, where there is a hatch that leads to the roof. There is a small parapet on the roof where I was able to safely hide without being detected. Every time a prostitute would lean into a car to discuss business I would pump up the air rifle two or three times and shoot her right in the ass. On most occasions she would slap the driver of the car, thinking that perhaps he had tried to sneak a quick pinch. I was careful so as not to pump up the air rifle more than two or three times or it could have inflicted some serious damage. I didn't want to hurt them, I just wanted them off my street," Jim chuckled. "And I did the same thing to the drug dealers as well," Jim went on. "Every time they would reach into their pocket to check their pagers or cell phones I would shoot them right in the hand. The beauty was that no one could find out where the shots were coming from! I spent many a weekend on my roof drinking beer and shooting hookers until the neighborhood was cleaned up."

STRANGE OCCURRENCES

Ever since Jim purchased his house he has experienced strange occurrences in his home. The very first incident occurred early one morning when Jim woke up to get ready for work. As he was getting ready to leave the house he could not find his keys anywhere. Every day after work he always placed his keys in a dish on a table by the front door, and that morning they were not there. Jim spent the next several weeks looking all over his house for his keys, but he was never able to find them. It was not until about three or four years later that he found the missing keys. Jim was under his house doing some work and he found the keys sitting on a sill beam underneath the crawl space. There was no logical explanation as to how his keys could have ended up there. This was the first occurrence that made Jim question if his house was haunted, but the activity in the home slowly began to escalate over the years.

It seemed that the spirits that haunt Jim's house like to move things around quite a bit. Jim once lost a pair of work boots, only to find them a few weeks later sitting on the mantle above the fireplace in his office. On numerous occasions Jim and his longtime girlfriend Marie have awakened to find all of the picture frames in the house have been tilted askew, as if someone had gone from room to room purposely making all of the pictures in the house crooked. On other occasions they have walked into the kitchen in the morning only to find that every single cabinet door was unexplainably opened. One night, while lying in bed together, Marie noticed that a hat hanging from the bedpost was spinning around by itself at an alarming rate, as if propelled by some unseen force. It seemed the most chilling occurrences in the home concerned the apparition of a young female who has been witnessed by more than one person over the years.

The infamous "Crazy Jim," who shot hookers from the roof of his home in the 1970s and early 1980s with a pellet gun to clean up the neighborhood.

The first time Jim saw her he had just come out of his upstairs bathroom. He saw the apparition of a young woman standing at the top of the stairs looking down. She appeared to be in her late teens, and she had her hair pinned up in the back. As soon as he opened the bathroom door she looked over her shoulder at him and then quickly darted down the hall and into the bedroom. As Jim put it, "It wasn't like she was walking, either; she was practically floating as she darted down the hall." The second time he saw her he was walking down his upstairs hallway when all of a sudden she came out of the upstairs bedroom, walked past him, and headed down the stairs.

A few years back Jim had some friends down for the weekend to enjoy the city's St. Patrick's Day festivities. One of his friends named John, who was one of his rocket buddies from Canada, had a strange experience at around 4:00 a.m. John was walking down the upstairs hallway to use the restroom when he noticed a beautiful young woman walking out of Jim's bedroom. The young woman walked down the staircase, opened the front door, and closed the door behind her as she left. Later that morning, as Jim was cooking breakfast for everyone, John approached him. "Jim, you dog! Who was that girl I saw leaving your bedroom earlier this morning?" Jim, who had been asleep in his room the night before with his girlfriend, asked, "Do you mean Marie?" "No," said John. "It wasn't Marie, and by the way, how did you talk Marie into that?" "I can assure you," replied Jim, "that there was no young girl in there with us last night. I'm quite sure that I would have remembered that. You must have seen the ghost."

After all that Jim has experienced since living there, it was not long before he asked Kim and I if we would be interested in investigating his house. Knowing that all three row houses (313–317 West Bolton Street) were built by the same person, I was excited to learn the history of our home, as well as Jim's. In addition, with all of the activity going on next door I could not pass up an opportunity like this.

THE HISTORY

According to historic maps of the city of Savannah, it is apparent a wooden structure that previously sat on the lot was torn down to construct what is now 313–317 West Bolton Street; 313 was constructed in 1888 by a building contractor named J. R. Eason, who owned J. R. Eason & Son. In 1890, he constructed 315 and 317 West Bolton Street. Throughout the 1890s, 315 West Bolton Street was the law offices of Wilson and Rogers, then it once again became a private residence throughout the early to mid-1900s. By the 1960s and 1970s, the building was used as two separate apartments, and Jim purchased the place in 1984. I was able to find numerous deaths in the home's history, but all were apparently from natural causes. As to whom the apparition of the woman was that kept appearing in Jim's house, it could have been any number of people, but for whatever reason this spirit was most definitely attached to this house.

THE INVESTIGATION

For years Jim and I had been trying to schedule a date to investigate his house, but with our busy schedules it was hard to find the time. In September 2014, Jim was out of town on a rocket launch and he gave me the keys to his house to keep an eye on the place. We both figured this was as good a time as any to set a date for an investigation. I arrived with Mandy and Kris Kersten one cold late September evening to investigate Jim's place. As soon as we arrived the air felt very dense, as if we were not alone, and a few minutes later I felt an extremely cold spot in the upstairs bathroom while conducting base readings. As I mentioned to Kris that I felt a cold spot my recorder caught a very clear recording of a female entity that asked, "Where at?" Perhaps this was the voice of the female who has been seen near the bathroom and the upstairs hall so many times before.

As the evening grew late, we three found ourselves conducting an EVP session in the upstairs front bedroom of the house. Mandy, who was seated closest to the door, heard heavy footsteps in the hall coming toward us. She quickly spun around and asked: "What the hell was that? That scared the hell out of me!" An audio recorder in the room caught a reply of a male spirit that answered, "Yeah, sorry." Evidently this spirit was somewhat remorseful for startling Mandy, who managed to hear more phantom footsteps later into the night. A few hours later she was walking down the staircase when all of a sudden footsteps came thudding down the stairs from behind her, yet Kris and I were already downstairs and no one else was in the house.

Aside from some great audio evidence, we documented some strange readings in electromagnetic activity (EMF), as well as some strange temperature drops. From what we could gather there are multiple spirits haunting Jim's house, male and female. But the question still remains: Who is the lady on the stairs and why does she still remain in this home? Maybe one day her identity will be discovered, but until then she will remain a mystery. Jim still experiences paranormal activity in his home on a regular basis, but as we all say about living in historic Savannah, "It comes with the territory." Besides, they were here long before us.

SHERMAN'S HOSPITAL

The Marshall House Hotel
Investigation

The Marshall House Hotel; unlike the 1860s, it does not cost an arm and a leg to stay there.

here are literally dozens of haunted hotels and inns in the historic district of Savannah, but few have a reputation for being more haunted than the Marshall House. Located on the east end of Broughton Street, this amazing building resembles something taken right off of Bourbon Street in New Orleans, Louisiana. The intricate wrought ironwork and old brick give the building a somewhat ominous feel. My paranormal research team had been trying to gain access to this location for nearly four years, and in October 2014, we were finally allowed to investigate the place. Over the years I have heard countless stories from guests on my tour that had experienced strange events while staying there and some of the reports from the staff were nothing short of horrifying.

THE HISTORY

I began each case as I always do, by researching the full history of the property at the Georgia Historical Society. Evidently, in the 1800s, a French cabinetmaker named Gabriel Leaver had bequeathed the land where the Marshall House now sits to his daughter, Mary Marshall. Soon after Mary decided she was going to use the land given to her to build a large family hotel. By 1851, the Marshall House Hotel was constructed as one of the finest hotels of its time, and the iron veranda was added five years later in 1856.

On December 21, 1864, Gen. William T. Sherman marched into Savannah with thousands of Union troops during the Civil War and captured the city, ending his famous "March to the Sea" which had begun in Atlanta six weeks before. Not long after he arrived he converted the Marshall House Hotel into a Civil War hospital for his wounded soldiers. The fact that there were already numerous beds in place made for a rather easy conversion. There was no doubt numerous deaths occurred there during Sherman's two-month stay in the city, many from amputations and surgeries that took place in the building. After Sherman left the city in early 1865, the Marshall House Hotel was later reopened again as a hotel.

In the early 1870s, the Florida House, which later became part of the Marshall House Hotel in 1880, was home to American journalist and folk writer Joel Chandler Harris for a brief while. Harris, who later became infamous for his *Uncle Remus* stories, met his wife in Savannah, and they were married in 1873. In 1877, Mary Marshall passed away at age ninety-three, leaving the hotel to a New Englander named William Coolidge.

By 1914, the building also housed a Woolworth's and a tailor shop. From the 1930s until the 1960s it served as a candy shop, a beauty shop, and a jewelry store in addition to the hotel. In 1957, the Marshall House Hotel finally closed its doors, and the building was then occupied by Blair's Shoe Repair, who remained there for many years. It was not until 1999, after extensive renovations to the structure, that it was once again reopened as the Marshall House Hotel, which continues to thrive today.

The hotel boasts such awards as one of *Coastal Living's* "Top 20 Places to Stay," as well as being listed in the Travel Channel's "Great Hotels" list. It has also been featured as a location in Telltale Games' hit *The Walking Dead*, but its name was changed to the Marsh House in the game for copyright reasons. In addition to its many accolades, there is also a darker side to the building. In 2005, the Travel Channel even featured the place on its *Haunted Hotels* program. For many years guests have reported such phenomena as hearing phantom children playing in the halls, seeing strange apparitions, and unexplainable smells of burning sulphur permeating the building. Some of the paranormal accounts from guests and employees who have stayed and worked at the Marshall House over the years are the most disturbing that I have ever heard about a hotel or inn in Savannah.

UNEXPLAINED BITE MARKS

One of the worst incidents happened to one of the first group of guests to stay in the hotel after its grand reopening. In early August 1999, a mother and her young daughter were some of the first to enjoy the new hotel and its upgraded amenities. Later in the evening the mother was sitting in bed, reading a book, when she began to hear her daughter talking to a little boy in the bathroom around the corner. The mother found this strange, considering the fact that she and her daughter were the only two people staying in the room that night. She walked into the bathroom and asked her daughter: "Who are you talking to sweetheart?" "I'm talking to the little boy in the bathtub mommy," replied the young girl. "Honey, there is no one in the bathtub," assured the mother. "Yes there is mommy, he's sitting right there! He has big teeth and he bit me!" The mother then saw the small teeth marks on her daughter's arm and quickly reported the incident to the hotel staff. In a separate incident involving similar activity the director of sales for the Marshall House, upon checking out one morning, noticed a small, round, mouth-shaped mark on her inner arm. The size of the mark was the size of a young child's mouth and there were individual teeth marks in the reddened circle.

On another occasion, a couple had checked in one afternoon and they were on the elevator headed up to their room on the third floor. When the elevator doors opened to the floor there was all out pandemonium from one end of the hall to the other. There were stretchers everywhere, and nurses and doctors were frantically running back and forth. The couple quickly returned downstairs and asked the manager if they happened to be filming a movie on the third floor. The manager looked at the couple strangely and informed them nothing of that nature was going on at the time in the hotel. When the couple returned to the third floor with the manager the floor looked as it should; just like any normal hotel hallway. Horrified by what they had just witnessed the couple left a few moments later to stay in a different hotel.

Only a few years back a man who was staying on the fourth floor reported seeing a little girl in a very dated, dingy white dress skipping down the hall behind him. The little girl beckoned to him, saying, "Come play with me." "I'm too busy," replied the man, who turned around and headed toward the elevator. He looked back for a moment, only to see that he was the only one standing in the long hallway. He had been alone the whole time.

In June 2004, one young woman had a strange encounter. She was lying in bed around midnight and was awakened by her boyfriend snoring loudly beside her. As she started to drift back to sleep, she suddenly felt something swoop down on to her chest. The pressure was heavy, as if a strong male had his knee to her chest, and one of her arms was pinned down, but she could not see anyone above her. She tried to scream but for some reason she could not speak. She tried to elbow her boyfriend, but her arm that was next to him was pinned down. When she reached across with her other arm something pushed that arm back to the bed. All of a sudden a raspy, angry male voice was in her face demanding to know, "Where is he?" The growling voice was then gone as quick as it had come. She was finally able to move and speak, and the only people in the room were her and her boyfriend. The following morning her shoulder still ached from where she had been grabbed during her encounter the night before.

In September 2005, one staff member recounted this horrifying encounter: "After turning down the bed one evening in a room on the fourth floor I noticed the apparition of a soldier suddenly appear. He was accompanied by the apparition of a small boy who was standing right beside him. The soldier glared right at me and said 'Get out of my room.' I left immediately."

THE WOMAN IN THE VEIL

In December 2007, a young woman staying on the fourth floor had a disturbing encounter. The woman had just locked the door to her room and was headed out to enjoy her afternoon. As she was walking down the hall toward the elevator she noticed a stern, elderly woman in an old white dress walking past her. The woman had a thin white veil covering her face from the eyes down. As she passed by the old woman turned to look at her with an angry scowl on her face and then disappeared. This very well could have been one of the nurses from the Union hospital still making her rounds.

Many of the accounts of the hauntings at the Marshall House Hotel have also come from guests staying there who have taken my ghost tour. In late spring 2014, I had a young couple from Russia on the tour that happened to be staying at the Marshall House. The young woman approached me between stops and told me of a strange dream she had the night before. Although it had been a dream, she felt that it had seemed all too real. She said: "I woke up in the middle of the night because I felt someone's fingers around my wrist and it was as if they were lightly lifting my arm and then gently letting it go. I slowly opened my eyes to see an older woman in a white dress who leaned over and gently put her wrinkled hand across my forehead and whispered 'Go back to sleep' in my ear."

I then asked the young woman if she knew the history of the Marshall House and she replied: "No, we just arrived late last night, and we have been out about town all day." I then went on to tell her about how the building had been used by Gen. Sherman during the Civil War as a hospital for his Union troops. I then told her that what she thought was a dream was possibly a real paranormal encounter. Perhaps the woman she had seen standing above her was in fact the ghost of a nurse from the old hospital, and the nurse was feeling her wrist as she was going around checking the pulses of her sleeping patients.

ROOM FOR ONE MORE

Another disturbing encounter happened a few months later in early July 2014. I received a call late one afternoon from two guests who had booked my ghost tour the day before. The woman on the phone said: "I need to call and cancel a tour that I booked with you yesterday. Before that, however, I would like to tell you the reason that we have decided to cancel. My husband and I arrived in town late last night without any hotel reservations and we checked into the Marshall House Hotel." With it being the off season I was sure that she would go on to tell me that there was plenty of room. "The lady behind the desk told us that there were only two rooms left, and that both rooms were very haunted," the woman continued. "I told her that we didn't believe much in ghosts and that we would settle for either room. Besides, we had been driving all day and I felt that by that point we could sleep through just about anything. 'After tonight you will be a believer,' the desk clerk then replied."

The woman said that she and her husband had found the statement a bit odd, but they retired to their room, exhausted from their long day of traveling. Later that evening they heard things in the room being moved about, and they even witnessed a smoky, gray apparition standing near their bed that night. The following morning the couple quickly sought out the hotel manager and began to tell him of the previous night's events, convinced that the lady behind the desk the night before had somehow set the whole thing up. The manager went on to tell the couple that there had been no woman working behind the desk that night, and furthermore, the couple was not even checked into the room in the hotel's computer system. After hearing this occurrence I completely understood why the couple was ready to call and cancel the ghost tour. They were supposed to spend a few days in Savannah, but after the previous night's events they left town early that morning. In fact, they were driving out of town as she was recounting her tale to me.

THE INVESTIGATION

In October 2014, I arrived just after midnight at the Marshall House Hotel with our equipment tech, Kris Kersten, to conduct our research of the building. Both of us had been amped up all week about the investigation, and as expected the Marshall House did not disappoint. We arrived and made room 423 on the top floor our home base and began to unpack. As soon as I could press record on my audio recorder we captured our first EVP; there was a very clear male voice on the playback that growled, "Where's Ryan Reese?" Reese, who had been my photographer in the group for the past three years, had just recently parted from the group not two weeks before to pursue other interests. I could not believe he was actually being called for by name!

Later in the evening we were able to document fairly high EMF (electromagnetic field) readings that we could not explain in the fourth floor hallway. At the same time one of these EMF spikes occurred an audio recorder picked up a strange EVP of a male spirit that growled, "Hurt them." Not long afterward another one was captured saying, "Get Ryan, get out." The voice that came through that time was absolutely chilling. Apparently we were dealing with some extremely angry spirits, and judging from the interviews we had conducted with employees and guests I was not surprised.

We were also able to document numerous strange anomalies with our REM pods during our investigation. A REM pod is a round disk with an antenna attached to it equipped with lights. When an electromagnetic field (EMF) is detected very near the antenna the pod will light up and make a noise, signifying the possible presence of a ghost. As with all EMF detectors and REM pods, you have to be very careful of false readings from natural EMF fields, but the readings we captured were completely unexplainable. On the third floor, as well as in the basement, we had the pods go off numerous times without a natural explanation, and many times in response to questions.

At around 3:00 a.m. we caught a strange recording on the fourth floor during an EVP session. One of our audio recorders captured the clear sound of a small female child moaning in the fourth floor hallway. There were no children in the hotel and this small voice sounded as if it was right next to us!

Out of all the areas of the hotel the top two floors seemed to be the most active, although we also had a few anomalous readings in the basement. As the hours went by and dawn soon approached, the investigation came to a close. We left the Marshall House with some chilling evidence, as well as the amazing feeling of knowing that after so many years we had finally had our chance to experience the hauntings there for ourselves. The staff still hear reports from guests quite often concerning ghostly encounters with the spirits that continue to haunt the building. The Marshall House Hotel may very well be one of the nicest stays in Savannah, but it is also definitely the most haunted.

CHAPTER 13

THE GHOST OF SARAH ANDERSON

The Ballastone Inn Investigation

Employees as well as guests have encountered a strange female apparition in period dress at the Ballastone Inn.

Just two houses down from Juliette Gordon Low's birthplace sits the graceful Ballastone Inn. At 14 East Oglethorpe Avenue, the home was essentially built for a Savannah planter named George Anderson and his wife Elizabeth in 1838. When George later died in 1847 at age seventy-nine due to declining health the home was left to his son, John W. Anderson, and his wife, Sarah. John, continuing in his father's footsteps, was also involved in the cotton industry as a cotton factor and merchant.

John and Sarah continued to live in the home until 1866, when John died at age sixty-one. Sarah passed away less than two years later in 1868 of ovarian cancer, and according to the inn's staff as well as guest reports, she is one of the resident ghosts of the home. Throughout the 1870s and early 1880s, the home was occupied by a commercial merchant named William Battersby. In 1888, Battersby sold the property to Capt. Henry Blun and his wife Catherine. The Bluns were immigrants from Germany who had arrived in the United States a few decades before in the 1850s. Capt. Blun had also served under Confederate Forces at Fort Pulaski just outside the city during the Civil War.

THE BLUN FAMILY

The Bluns were quite a large family, boasting twelve children: six boys and six girls. This explains why Mr. Blun later had his home enlarged, enlisting prominent Boston architect William Gibbons Preston to complete the task. The Bluns continued to thrive in Savannah until tragedy struck less than a month before Christmas 1875. One of the Blun children—twelve-year-old Margaret, affectionately known as "Margo"—became sick with varioloid (a mild form of smallpox usually found in patients who have either previously had the disease or had been vaccinated for it in the past). After weeks of battling the virus young Margo finally departed from this world on December 5, 1875, leaving the Bluns to face a rather somber holiday season.

On February 12, 1912, Henry Blun was found dead in his bed of old age in what is now known as the Oglethorpe Room of the inn. His wife, Catherine, continued to live in the home for another ten years until she finally joined her husband in September 1922. The home changed ownership quite a few times throughout the next decade until it was spilt up into separate rental apartments in 1932, known as the Lester House.

Owned by a barber named John Lester Wyatt and his wife, Alberta, the Lester House continued to thrive until 1947, when it was then renamed Troy Apartments. According to city directories over the next twenty-two years, the Troy Apartments were split into eighteen separate rental units, which had several new tenants almost every year.

By the 1970s, the home was used as overflow and storage for the adjacent Juliette Gordon Low Birthplace Museum until the 1980s. In 1980, it was finally converted into the beautiful bed and breakfast which now exists as the Ballastone Inn. In 2002, Jennifer Salandi, the current owner, purchased the property, but little did she know that she was also acquiring the spirits that were attached to the home. According to Jennifer, the ghosts here are friendly in nature. While employees and guests have had numerous encounters with the paranormal, there have never been any unfriendly encounters.

Guests staying at the inn customarily inform the staff that they have felt a light touch on the shoulder while walking down the hall, only to turn around to see no one there. After recounting their experience most determine it was a female presence they had encountered due to the light feminine touch on the shoulder. This very well may be the ghost of Sarah Anderson, who has been seen throughout the home over the years by staff and guests. Contrary to popular myth ghosts can be seen during daytime as well as night, and Mrs. Anderson usually chooses to appear during the day.

Although it is full of friendly spirits, the guests staying at the Ballastone Inn have had numerous strange experiences there over the years.

WALKING THROUGH WALLS

One of the most interesting sightings of Sarah Anderson occurred one late afternoon a few years back. The inn's head housekeeper was in the elevator, headed up to the fourth floor to check on a room. As the elevator doors opened she saw the apparition of a woman in period dress with her hair tied into a tight grey bun standing in the hall. When the woman saw the elevator doors open she glanced briefly at the head housekeeper, then quickly darted into the Gazebo Room. The housekeeper then hurriedly entered the room directly across the hall and glanced into the Gazebo Room. As she did the female entity walked directly into the side of the wall in the room and disappeared. It was later determined that the housekeeper had encountered the ghost of Sarah Anderson.

One afternoon numerous employees witnessed this same female spirit while in the main lobby of the inn. As a few of the staff were gathered around the main desk in the lobby a tall woman in a big skirt and high-collared shirt walked right through the front door. She had her grey hair tied up in a tight grey bun as she walked into the front entranceway. The alarming part of this was that she had literally walked through the front door of the home without actually opening the door! The strange apparition then took a right into the parlor as she was followed by the employees, who were still astounded by what they had just witnessed. As the staff entered the parlor they were even more taken aback because the parlor in which the woman had just entered was now completely empty.

Although Mrs. Anderson almost always chooses to appear during the day, there was one occurrence in which she came back to visit in the evening. There were two ladies who happened to be staying in the Gazebo Room a few years ago that had a strange encounter with the resident ghost. One of the ladies was downstairs in the front parlor, waiting on her friend to finish getting ready. The other woman was in the room, seated at the vanity and doing her makeup. As she was looking in the mirror she saw a woman in a long white night shirt walk right behind her. This woman appeared to be in her late fifties to early sixties, and as usual, she had her hair tied up in a tight grey bun. When the woman seated at the vanity quickly turned around there was no one behind her and the room was completely empty save for herself.

According to Jennifer Salandi, they receive hundreds of calls and emails each month from paranormal investigation groups all over the United States who want to investigate the property. In January 2015, our team was the first to be allowed overnight access to conduct a paranormal investigation, and to this day I still can't thank Jennifer enough for allowing us to investigate her beautiful inn. When I arrived just after 8:00 p.m. that evening with investigators Kris and Mandy Kersten, I was already filled with anticipation and the excitement of finally being allowed to investigate the home after all these years.

THE INVESTIGATION

As soon as we arrived we used the front left tea room as main base and began unpacking our equipment. I had just turned on a REM pod, placed it on a nearby table, and returned to unpacking. Within less than a minute the pod began to go off. There was no one near it, nor any other disturbances that could account for the anomaly. It seemed the spirits in the building were already ready to communicate. After the REM pod incident we finished unpacking and conducted our initial base readings, then we decided to all three split up to cover more ground.

While in the room known as the Gazebo Room I captured an awesome EVP almost as soon as I started asking questions. After the third or fourth question I asked, "Is there anyone in the room here with me?" Right afterward I caught a clear response from a young girl who answered, "Margo." This was the same name of Henry Blun's daughter that had died in the building almost 140 years before! We had not even been in the home for an hour and I had captured a name that matched a death in the home. Later into the investigation, while in that same room, both Kris and his wife Mandy witnessed a tall, dark, three-dimensional shadow figure dart from behind them and then quickly disappear into the wall. Being that Sarah Anderson has been the only reported sighting of a ghost in the inn, this may very well have been her spirit that the Kerstens witnessed.

After a few hours, we were all three standing outside the inn, just under the front parlor window getting some fresh air, when all of a sudden Mandy shouted, "What in the hell was that?" As we turned around to see what was going on Mandy was pointing at the parlor window. "Someone was just standing there watching us outside that window and they disappeared," exclaimed Mandy. "It was a tall dark figure, and it had been watching us while we were outside." After this we were all a little apprehensive about going back into the building to continue the investigation, but our break was over and we still had quite a lot of ground left to cover.

Although we had experienced the majority of the activity throughout the night in the Gazebo Room, a strange occurrence happened not long before midnight in the Low Country Room. The three of us were seated on the bed conducting an EVP session when Mandy and I felt something brush past both of our arms. The room then became extremely cold and we documented a sudden eight degree temperature drop. A smell of mentholated medicine then began to fill the room, yet there was no logical explanation as to where the smell may have come from. Later on I asked, "Do you want us to leave?" and a spirit quickly replied, "Go."

Before concluding the investigation for the night we decided to go back to the Gazebo Room one last time, since it seemed to be the most active room in the building. After about ten minutes a REM pod which had been placed on the bed began to light up. At the same time my Mel-meter documented an unexplainable 7.3 milligauss spike and the temperature in the room began to drop significantly. About four minutes later a loud knocking sound began from outside the far window. As we went to the window to investigate the strange noise the sound became louder. As I opened the curtain and looked out the window I realized that we were on the top floor of the inn, and that there was nothing outside to account for the sound. At the same time the knocking sound began a strange female moan was captured on Kris's audio recorder that sounded like a woman in pain. The strange knocking sound then began to escalate in volume and stopped almost as quickly as it had started.

Throughout the rest of the investigation the home remained rather quiet. It was almost as if the spirits had expelled their energy by communicating with us during the onset of the night. Although the activity had quieted down early that evening, we were still quite pleased with the results of our findings.

To this day guests report odd occurrences while staying at the Ballastone Inn, yet the spirits here seem to be happy with their surroundings. Perhaps it is because Jennifer has painstakingly decorated every square inch of the home with beautiful antique furnishings that make the place come alive with true Southern charm. Her meticulous eye for detail ensures that every guest feels at home while visiting our beautiful city. Perhaps if you are lucky you may even encounter the ghost of Sarah Anderson, who still continues to walk the halls of her old home.

⥥ A LINK TO THE PAST

The Crystal Beer Parlor Investigation

The Crystal Beer Parlor is home to the best peach cobbler in the state of Georgia as well as the home of numerous ghosts.

Nestled on the corners of Jefferson and West Jones Street, the Crystal Beer Parlor has been serving up mouth-watering burgers, hand cut fries, and of course ice cold beers for over eighty years. Opened the year that prohibition ended in 1933, the Crystal Beer Parlor derived its name from the Crystal Ice Company that used to sit just across the street. The current owner, John Nichols, has fond memories of having milkshakes and burgers there quite often as a young child. When John purchased the restaurant in 2010, he incorporated many of the old menu items that Savannahians remembered all too well, in addition to adding some new dishes, many of which showcase John's Greek heritage.

THE HISTORY

Years before the building that now sits at 301 West Jones Street as the Crystal Beer Parlor was constructed, Savannah city maps show three wooden buildings used to exist on the lot. These structures were built in 1888, for a man named S. C. Dunning. By 1899, Henry Lowry, a bicycle dealer, is listed as living in the home. From 1904 to 1906, John and Lula Humphrey operated their stove repair business in the building, as well as lived there. Over the next couple of years a woodworker named George Anderson lived in the home with his wife Bessie until 1910. That year the brick building that now sits at 301 West Jones Street was constructed for a man named Henry Gerken. It was opened that year as the Gerken Family Grocery Store, which was operated by a man named Julius Weitz. Mr. Weitz lived on the second floor of the building right above the store with his wife and young children.

By 1929, the Gerken Family Grocery Store had closed and the building remained vacant until 1933. In 1933, William "Blocko" Manning and his wife Connie purchased the property and opened the Crystal Beer Parlor. Although the property has changed hands a few times over the years, it has continued to remain one of the most popular family restaurants in the city. The menu boasts old classics, such as their creamy crab stew and the hamburger steak with onions, as well as new favorites, such as the Brown Ale Burger and the "Greek Taco," which is their unique take on the traditional gyro.

Whether taking my family out to a nice afternoon lunch or joining a friend for a cold beer and a football game at the bar, this place has been one of my "go to" restaurants for quite a while. Although I have been frequenting the place since 2010, it was not until fall 2014 that I heard about the hauntings that took place there. One of my good friends, Rose Gillespie (who is also mentioned in *Savannah's Afterlife* in the "Boar's Head Restaurant" story), had just started working at the Crystal Beer Parlor less than a month before when she began to hear ghost stories from the staff. Evidently the place had been haunted for years, and Rose contacted me soon after to see if our paranormal research team would be interested in investigating the property. Naturally I jumped at the opportunity, and in less than a week I was seated at a table with the restaurant's owner, John Nichols, discussing the paranormal activity that occurs in the building.

THE HAUNTINGS

The two of us were joined by Paige Brown, the restaurant's general manager, and Gail Lusk, the marketing investor. Gail also lived upstairs on the second floor in the apartment that the Weitz family formerly occupied. According to John, the activity in the building began the very first day he reopened the restaurant. As John was walking down the hall an old pay phone in the hallway began to ring. When John answered it there was nothing but dead silence on the other end of the line. The most unnerving part is the fact that the phone had been disconnected many years before. John felt the spirits in the building may have been calling to thank him for reopening the restaurant, and as far as he knows the phone has not rang again since that day. This apparently has not been the first strange incident to occur near the old pay phone. A previous owner of the restaurant reported seeing a strange apparition of a man in a cowboy hat leaning against the wall one evening. The man was standing beside the pay phone for a moment, then he suddenly vanished.

One of the more terrifying encounters happened to a previous general manager who was standing beside the pay phone while adjusting the thermostat late one night after closing up. The manager happened to look to his left at a picture frame hanging on the wall beside the thermostat and saw a frightening sight. In the reflection of the frame's glass he could see an old woman was standing in the dining room directly behind him, glaring intently in his direction. The manager then quickly spun around, only to find that the dining room was completely empty.

Other strange activity that occurs on the first floor of the building happens in the women's restroom. There have been many instances in which women have run out of the restroom screaming hysterically. Once they have calmed down they begin to describe being in the middle stall of the restroom, then all of a sudden seeing a large black mass near the top of the adjacent stall. This black form then proceeds to crawl over the top of the stall toward them, as if to envelop them into its dark matter. The women are then seen running out of the restroom, horrified by the lurking presence they had just nearly escaped.

GAIL'S APARTMENT

Although John and Paige had experienced odd occurrences in the building, it was Gail Lusk who had more encounters with the spirits than anyone else in the restaurant. It seemed that despite the fact that the first floor had a lot of strange activity, it was Gail's apartment that was the most haunted area of the building. She had moved into the apartment less than a year before, and upon moving in Gail said that something about the place just did not feel right. There was a heavy presence surrounding the apartment, but after renovating the place and making it her own the dense feeling went away and has not since returned. The ghosts that haunt the apartment have never left.

Most of the activity occurs in Gail's bedroom, and strangely enough, it happens most often on Thursday nights. Gail does the marketing for the Crystal Beer Parlor, and on Thursday nights she lines out all of the marketing materials on her bed to put the packets together. One Thursday evening Gail was sitting on the edge of her bed when she suddenly felt someone sit down on the other side, yet she was the only one in the room. There was then a loud thud on the floor, although nothing had fallen. According to Gail, it sounded as if someone were sitting on the edge of the bed, taking off their heavy leather work boots and dropping them on to the hardwood floor before retiring for the night.

A few weeks later Gail was lying in bed late one evening when she had a chilling encounter. Just moments before drifting off to sleep she felt someone crawl into bed beside her, yet she was the only one in the room. As Gail described the incident, she felt the entity that had crawled in bed with her was most likely a small, scared little child, possibly a timid young female spirit. Gail did not feel threatened by the encounter, yet she felt as if this spirit were trying to gain comfort by crawling into bed with her. This child entity may also be the reason that Gail finds her slippers sitting directly under the bed in the middle almost every morning when she wakes, yet she always places them right beside her bed every night before going to sleep.

THE INVESTIGATION

After listening to John, Paige, and Gail describe in detail all of the strange encounters in the building we set a date for the investigation for mid-February of the upcoming year. When we arrived that night to begin our research, I was thrilled to know that not only would we be allowed to investigate the whole restaurant, but Gail was gracious enough to allow us to investigate the upstairs apartment as well. As soon as we entered Gail's apartment an EVP was captured in her bedroom of a small child clearly laughing. This may very well have been the same child that Gail had encountered a few months before in her bed. A few minutes later one of the most disturbing audio recordings of the investigation was caught in the same room, an EVP that said, "There's ghosts here," as if to inform us that we were definitely not alone. About a minute later the doors to the armoire in Gail's bedroom were wide open, as if something had opened them to prove its presence in the room. These are heavy wooden doors that are not prone to opening by themselves.

As the evening progressed the atmosphere in the restaurant began to feel more heavy and thick by the moment, and we could tell that there was an unseen presence all around us. Later on in the night I was seated at a table with Kris Kersten and Paige conducting an EVP session when all of a sudden we captured a clear recording of a man who shouted: "Ya'll ain't from around here!" At about the same time Mandy came running out of the women's restroom, proclaiming: "You aren't going to believe what just happened in there!" Mandy started explaining how she had been in the middle stall of the women's restroom conducting an EVP session. The stall door was shut and latched, yet out of nowhere the handle on the latch started jiggling and the door started shaking back and forth, as if something were trying to jerk the door open. Mandy unlatched the stall door and proceeded to run out of the restroom, and that is when she joined back up with us.

A little bit before 2:00 a.m. I had walked outside with Kris, Mandy, and Paige to get some fresh air. The three of us had been standing just outside the parking lot entrance to the restaurant, conversing about the success of the investigation thus far. Upon reentering the building Paige immediately stopped dead in her tracks. "What was that?" she shouted. She went on to explain how she had just seen a tall shadow figure dart directly in front of the door to the women's restroom and then disappear. Perhaps this was the same dark shadow that has been witnessed many times before lurking over the top of the middle stall. While we were outside I had left a stationary recorder on a small table in the entrance way near the bathrooms. Just before we had reentered the building and Paige had witnessed the shadow figure that recorder had captured the sound of heavy footsteps and someone moving about, yet we were all still outside the restaurant. At around 3:00 a.m., things had died down for quite a while and we decided to conclude our investigation. We still had a ton of evidence to go through and it seemed that the spirits in the restaurant had finally exhausted themselves.

I still frequent the Crystal Beer Parlor quite often; these guys have been serving up great food for over eighty years. The warm atmosphere and inviting staff make it one of the best restaurants in town. The walls are lined with old photographs and newspaper clippings highlighting Savannah's historic past, and they even have a special beer list dedicated to the "Beers of our Fathers." This includes the stuff we remember snagging out of our pop's fridge when he wasn't looking, such as Genesee Cream Ale, Lone Star, and Iron City Beer, just to name a few. Do not worry hopheads, they have another full beer menu dedicated to the newly revived art of craft beers too. Be sure to try the duck wings; they are not on the menu, but they have them most days—you just have to ask your server (our little secret). Don't forget to save room for dessert, because not only are they one of the few restaurants that serve peach cobbler in downtown Savannah (which is surprising, since we are considered the Peach State), but they have perhaps the best that I have ever tasted.

CHAPTER 15

HILBO'S GHOST

The Alligator Soul Restaurant
Investigation

Alligator Soul, where love prevails, even beyond the veil of death.

Just off the north end of Telfair Square, where I begin my tour every night, sits the Alligator Soul Restaurant. Although the restaurant began in Seattle, Washington, the Savannah location was opened at 114 Barnard Street in 2003 by owners Hilbo and Maureen Craig. Maureen lost her husband, Hilbo, to lung cancer in 2007, but she continues to operate the restaurant, adhering to the same attention to detail set forth by her and Hilbo years before. Known for their traditional fine dining with a creole flare, Alligator Soul is, in my opinion, hands down the best gourmet restaurant in town. Now led by culinary wizard

Chef Stephen McClain and his team, they are known throughout the area for their handmade artisan breads, house-cured meats, and adventurous game, which are all sourced through organic and local sources.

WHAT'S IN A NAME?

When selecting the name Alligator Soul for their restaurant, Chef Hilbo and Maureen had a deeper meaning in mind. The alligator represents a person's exterior. Although an alligator may seem hard and impenetrable on the exterior, it is what is on the inside that matters. The soul part of the name represents what is on the interior—your true nature. As the old adage goes, "It's what's on the inside that counts." The Craigs have always held integrity in very high regards, and according to Maureen, this sums up entirely their meaning behind the unique name.

THE HISTORY

Although the Craigs opened the restaurant in Savannah in 2003, the history of the building in which Alligator Soul now resides dates back much farther. In 1888, 114 Barnard Street was built for Henry and Amelia Haym. The Hayms, who were immigrants from Prussia, had raised seven children, one of which died twenty-eight years earlier in 1860. Joseph Henry Haym had been declared dead at the Haym's previous home on August 16, 1850, from a condition known as marasmus, a form of severe malnutrition caused by energy deficiency. The disease is characterized by loss of muscle, a shrunken, wasted appearance, ear and throat infections, and bloody stool. If not treated, the body eventually loses its ability to synthesize proteins and the patient eventually dies. Poor Joseph's condition went untreated and he died at less than a year old.

In January 1904, Amelia Haym was declared dead in her room from injuries she received from falling down the stairs just a few days before; she was seventy-seven years old. By the following year, the building was converted into the Southern Grocery Company, owned by Mr. L. W. Roberts. The store only lasted a couple of years, because by 1908, Mr. I. Clinton Helmy and his wife Clara lived in the building. They also operated the I. C. Helmy Furniture Company from their home until the early 1920s. In 1922, the Savannah Gas Company occupied the building, where they remained for over seventy years until the mid-1990s. Stanley Friedman lived there for the next few years, where he also operated Friedman and Martin Law Offices, until Hilbo and Maureen Craig purchased the building in 2003. Although the restaurant may have some residual hauntings from previous tenants, it is the ghost of Chef Hilbo Craig that most people have encountered. Although Hilbo did not actually die in the restaurant, it is no wonder why he has chosen to spend most of his time in the afterlife there. This place was his pride and joy, and Maureen feels that Hilbo is still there, popping in to visit her from time to time.

Maureen is not the only one who has encountered Hilbo's ghost. Jason Johns, the restaurant's general manager, has had quite a few experiences in the building. One stormy evening a few years ago something had caused the security lights that lead up to the back stairway to go out, as well as the main flood light at the top of the staircase. Jason and another employee were standing at the top of the stairs, looking out the back door and watching the thunderstorm, and by that point it was really coming down hard. As the two of them started back down the stairs there was a loud crack of lightning and the lights leading up the stairs came back on one by one in succession. Then, as the main flood light at the top of the stairs clicked back on the song in the restaurant's playlist suddenly changed. Chef Hilbo used to sing gospel, and it was one of his gospel songs that started blaring through the restaurant's speakers. The odd thing was that Jason's iPhone® was plugged into the dock and he did not have any of Hilbo's songs on his playlist, yet somehow it was now coming through the speakers at a high volume.

A few months later, Jason was locking up the restaurant and he was the last one in the place. After he had turned all of the lights out he was getting ready to set the alarm before exiting the building. Out of the corner of his eye he noticed a large white figure darting past the fireplace. It was a rounded figure, and it had a tall white chef's hat on. As soon as he saw it, it disappeared. Jason believes that this may have been the ghost of Maureen's late husband, Chef Hilbo Craig.

TABLE 23

Other strange occurrences have centered around what is known as table number 23. About a year ago, for almost a week strange things would happen at only that table. Every time a server tried to place silverware on it the pieces would slide together and not stay in position. Jason and other staff members would try different pieces of silverware with the same result. They would then experiment by trying it on different tables with no movement whatsoever. It seemed that table 23 was the only table where this would happen. After about a week the problem did not occur again. "We tried not to seat anyone at that table that week unless we absolutely had to," said Jason regarding the incident.

One of the other odd occurrences in the restaurant happens to Maureen quite often when she arrives to work early in the morning. Maureen is almost always the first to arrive at work, and everyone else usually comes in a few hours later. There have been many mornings in which she has heard someone whistling a tune in the back service area, yet she is the only one there. Maureen says that it is always the same voice and tune, yet she has not been able to place what it is that this spirit is whistling. Other employees have reported the feeling of someone standing directly over their shoulder, only to turn around to find that no one is there.

The lounge area of Alligator Soul, where the apparition in the chair appeared during our investigation.

THE INVESTIGATION

When we arrived one cold February evening in 2015 to investigate the restaurant, I do not think any of us were quite sure what to expect. Of course, we were hoping to communicate with the spirits tied to the building's history, but it was Chef Hilbo that I was most interested in communicating with. I was hoping to get some kind of sign that he was still around for Maureen. I can't imagine ever losing my wife, and I know how hard it must be for Maureen. If I would be able to get any evidence that Hilbo was still around, perhaps it would help Maureen in some way. I had no idea that his spirit would come through in the way it did.

Throughout the investigation we managed to capture some amazing EVPs, but there were two in particular that absolutely blew my mind. A few weeks after we had finished up the investigation at Alligator Soul I was at home, typing up the rest of the case files, when Kris Kersten, our equipment tech, dropped by. Kris had just finished reviewing his audio, and he had captured two strange EVPs. A few hours into the investigation we had been in the back hallway, conducting an EVP session, and Kris had asked, "What is your name?" On the playback a male voice clearly replied, "Hilary." "I've been through the history over and over, but I can't find the name Hilary anywhere," Kris said. At that very moment chills ran down my spine.

I looked at Kris and explained to him that Hilbo Craig's real name was Hilary Craig. He had gone by the nickname Hilbo and was seldom referred to as Hilary. There was no way that Kris could have known this, and we had it on audio recording! On the same recording less than twenty minutes later, we were conducting an EVP session in the lounge area and I had asked: "If there are any other spirits here can you tell us their name?" A female voice clearly replied with, "Hilary." It seemed the ghost of Chef Craig was still in the building, as well as another female presence.

THE APPARITION IN THE CHAIR

One of the more disturbing incidents happened later that night as I was walking through the doorway from the service area to the dining room. As I rounded the corner I saw the silhouettes of what appeared to be Kris and Mandy sitting in the lounge area. We had been lights out for a few hours by that point and all I could see was their shadows. Mandy was seated on the couch facing my direction and Kris was in the lounge chair with his back to me. Knowing that we were the only three people locked in the building at that point I thought we were all accounted for. I saw Kris turn around in the chair and look at me, but as I got closer, the figure in the chair that I had mistaken for Kris suddenly disappeared. At that moment I saw Kris come walking out of the dining room to my right. Whatever was in the chair was now gone, and Mandy and Kris had not seen a thing. This entity had looked directly at me before it decided to disappear, leading to the assumption that this was indeed an intelligent spirit.

In addition to the personal experiences and the audio evidence we experienced quite a few high spikes on our EMF detectors throughout the night, including one in the small dining room that was over twenty milligauss. Out of everything we experienced on the investigation though, it is the "Hilary" EVP that still astounds me. If anything else, we were able to capture evidence that Hilbo is still around, and he seems happy at his restaurant, spending his days with his lovely wife. When you visit, be sure to try his signature dish, the "Little Hilbo." Do not let the name fool you, there is nothing little about this dish. It is a cold-smoked, dry-aged, Cajun-rubbed, sixteen-ounce ribeye steak topped with a veal demi-glace and a bourbon peppercorn cream sauce, served with duck fat frites and fresh vegetables. This amazing dish of Chef Craig's has not changed since he created it years ago. Also check and see what creative dish Chef McClain has whipped up; I have managed to try everything from antelope, kangaroo, and turtle to gator here. Regardless of the dish you choose, rest assured you are in good hands. There is nothing short of an amazing meal to be had at Alligator Soul.

CHAPTER 16

THE OLD CARRIAGE DEALER

The Churchill's Pub
Investigation

The building that houses Churchill's Pub was originally built in 1869 for a
carriage dealer named Solomon Cohen.

For years Churchill's Pub has been my local watering hole. Most nights after finishing my tours I pop in for a quick "traveler." For those of you not familiar with Savannah's Historic District, it is one of the very few areas in the United States that allows you to take an alcoholic beverage along with you down the street wherever you go. These are commonly referred to as "travelers," or "go cups." As Joe Odom stated best in John Berendt's *Midnight in the Garden of Good and Evil*, "If you have to leave the party, you always take a traveler."After a night of tours nothing is better than a cold I.P.A. for the walk home.

BOB AND MICHELLE

More often than not, as soon as I enter Churchill's I am greeted by Bob and Michelle Masteller, who have been working there together since Michelle hired Bob over eight years ago. Not long after the hiring the two began dating and they have now been married for several years. The duo works together four nights a week behind the bar, and you would be hard-pressed to find better bar service anywhere in town. I have seen ghost tours stop by the pub numerous times, and one night, as she was pouring my traveler, I casually asked Michelle if the place was haunted. Being a tour guide and paranormal investigator for the past few years in Savannah I had not heard any stories about the old pub. "Some say that it is, but I haven't experienced anything," replied Michelle. She then went on to tell me about how numerous guests and staff had reported strange experiences in the women's restroom in the basement, but other than that she had not heard much else.

With the building being in the oldest section of the city I was sure it had to have its own rich history. I mentioned to Michelle in passing that if they ever wanted us to investigate the building we would love to check it out. Less than two weeks later she had spoken with the owner, Andy Holmes, who readily agreed to allow us overnight access to conduct an investigation. Having been a patron of the pub for years I was excited to gain overnight access, but at the same time I was ambivalent as to how the results of our research would turn out. There were scant stories here and there of hauntings, but not as many as we were used to. Little did I know that the property was much more haunted than we could have ever imagined.

A lady came up to me one day and said, "Sir! You are drunk," to which I replied, "I am drunk today madam, and tomorrow I shall be sober but you will still be ugly."
–Winston Churchill

Be sure to ask for Bob and Michelle while visiting Churchill's Pub. You would be hard-pressed to find better bartenders anywhere in town.

THE HISTORY

Churchill's is in the oldest section of town at 13 West Bay Street, right next door to the infamously haunted Moon River Brewing Company. The structure was built in 1869 for Solomon and Miriam Cohen after a fire earlier in January that year destroyed their home that had existed on the same lot. Mr. Cohen was a carriage dealer and a postmaster, and Miriam took care of the Cohen's three children: Gratz, Belle, and Miriam Cohen Jr. On August 14, 1875, only six years after the current structure was finished, Solomon Cohen died of old age. The building then remained vacant over the next twenty years until 1897, when it was reopened as M.S. & D.A. Byck Stationers and Printers, owned by brothers Moses and David Byck.

The Byck brothers only owned the building for a few years, then, in the early 1900s, the Savannah Coca-Cola Bottling Company occupied the property. After a few short years the L. R. Myers Cigar Company took over occupancy of the building, where they remained until the late 1920s. Over the next few decades the building was owned by an electric company, an elevator company, and a whole mill supply and machine store. By the late 1970s and early 1980s, it had become vacant, then it went on to become a myriad of bars and nightclubs, including a couch bar in the 1990s. In 2004, Andy Holmes relocated Churchill's Pub from its previous location on Drayton Street into the building, and it has remained there ever since.

THE INVESTIGATION

When I arrived on March 1, 2015, with investigators Kris and Mandy Kersten we began to experience strange occurrences almost immediately. As I was conducting base readings on the second floor in the private dining area known as 10 Downing my Mel-meter caught a sudden 56.5 milligauss spike near the bar. The spike came and went immediately and could not be replicated by natural phenomenon, leading me to believe this to be a paranormal encounter. These were extremely high levels of EMF, but later into the night another Mel-meter spike was caught in the basement area known as Winston's, the section of the restaurant reserved for a wine bar and private dining events. Near the benches in Winston's a 130 milligauss EMF spike was captured that could not be explained. Not only are these high levels of EMF energy, but we could not find anything in the building that could be causing these high readings naturally.

A few hours later I was in the women's restroom in the basement with Kris and Mandy, and we had just turned all the lights out. Mandy was standing in the doorway leading to the hall when Kris's audio recorder captured a chilling EVP of a male entity that growled, "Shut the door, Mandy." Whoever it was, they did not sound a bit happy. Evidently they wanted us shut in the room with them, and they were not in the least bit shy about voicing their opinion. A little while later things really started to pick up.

The beautiful bar that sits in Churchill's was actually imported from England, which adds to the pub's authenticity for everything British.

Just after 6:00 a.m., I was in the basement, seated at a table with Kris and Mandy. We were exhausted from the investigation and we were beginning to wrap things up when all of a sudden we heard loud footsteps tramping back and forth above us across the wooden floors. It sounded like multiple people were walking around directly above us, yet we were the only three people in the building. We decided to do a final EVP session before packing up and that is when things got even more strange.

I had placed a REM pod on a bar stool in Winston's to try and detect spirit activity. I asked: "Can you sit down at that bar stool?" in hopes that a spirit would go near the REM pod and make it light up. Right afterward my audio recorder captured an EVP of a female spirit that clearly responded: "I'm over here where the bar stool is." Evidently there were intelligent spirits haunting this pub, since I was able to get a direct Class A response to my question.

About ten minutes later Mandy was seated across from Kris and I at a table in the basement, and she had her left foot stretched out beside her on the bench. As we were conducting an EVP session Kris saw a small shadow figure near Mandy's outstretched foot. The figure suddenly disappeared, and then all three of us witnessed a small indentation appear on the cushion near Mandy's foot, as if something had just sat down right beside her. Mandy then felt icy cold fingers grasp her outstretched

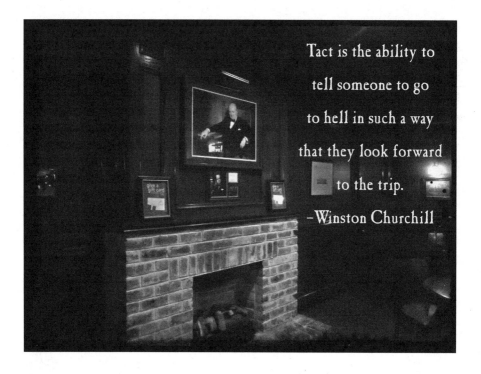

Tact is the ability to tell someone to go to hell in such a way that they look forward to the trip.
-Winston Churchill

The dining room at Churchill's may seem inviting, but you never know what may be lurking just around the corner.

ankle and give it a good jerk. Kris and I watched in astonishment as the whole incident happened right before our eyes, while Mandy sat right across from us, frozen with fear from the dark encounter. Right afterward the footsteps above us stopped, and we did not catch anything else. It was almost as if whatever it was in the building had used the last of its energy to make physical contact with Mandy.

Although initially I may have had my doubts as to the paranormal activity occurring at Churchill's Pub, after our investigation of the building I was quite sure the place was most definitely haunted. The sheer magnitude of the EMF spikes were astonishing enough, but some of the EVPs we managed to capture, in addition to Mandy's chilling basement experience, absolutely blew my mind. Now that I was able to experience the building on an overnight investigation, I am actually quite surprised that there are not more reports of paranormal occurrences in the place. Churchill's will continue to be one of my favorite bars in town, and when I am in the mood for some traditional, authentic English fare there is no place better. A lot of the kitchen guys are from Manchester and they make a mean steak and ale pie. If you are feeling rather adventurous add a side of Manchester Caviar (English for mushy peas), they are quite delicious!

The three scratches that appeared on Kristen Haglund were believed to be caused by a demonic entity. In many cases attacks by demonic spirits appear with scratches in groups of three. This is usually a sign that the evil presence is trying to mock the Holy Trinity.

The Savannah Ghost Research Society has been conducting paranormal research for quite a while now, and one of the questions I hear more often than anything else is, "What is the worst case that you have encountered?" Being that our team has spent the night in some of the most haunted locations in the United States, it is always hard to answer that question with only one haunted location in mind. That was until I received a phone call in mid-March 2015 from Scott Haglund. Little did I know that this particular phone call would lead to the most disturbing case our team has ever handled.

A FRIGHTENING CALL

I was in the office early one afternoon finishing up typing the case files from our Churchill's Pub investigation we had done just a few weeks before when the telephone rang. The gentleman on the other end of the line introduced himself as Scott Haglund, and he was a paranormal investigator from Long Island, New York. His daughter, Kristin, was a student at the Savannah College of Art and Design, and she was experiencing extremely disturbing occurrences in her home. She, along with her roommates Linsay Hubbard and Stacie Gilbert, had been renting a house on West 35th Street for over a year and a half, and just recently they had started to experience strange activity in the home. A few months before a power surge had occurred on their block and that is when the haunting began.

The strange thing about this particular case was the fact that we could find no prior history tied to the property that could explain the experiences the girls were having. The home was built in 2002, and had changed hands a few times over the years through various property rental agencies, yet there were no documented deaths or anything else that we usually find attached to haunted locations. In addition, there was not much in the way of anything tied to the land that the house sat on either. The home was located in a bad section of town and it had remained vacant for a couple years, so who knows what may have happened in the building during those unoccupied years. Another theory suggests that maybe a previous tenant had experimented with the occult and had possibly opened some sort of portal that had not been properly closed. In any instance, the activity these girls were experiencing was nothing short of horrifying.

It had all started with little things here and there, such as footsteps heard pacing back and forth in the attic and strange voices heard when no one else was around. Soon after the iPhones® of all three girls would often have complete battery drains, even when their phones were fully charged. Although it began innocently enough, it very quickly escalated into much darker territory. Stacie would see a small, dark, demonic looking figure crouching down in her room, and Linsay would see a tall thin man in a dark suit and wide-brimmed hat come out of her closet at night when she slept. The dogs in the house began to act strange, as if there was someone in the house the girls could not see. The animals would constantly bark at one particular corner of the living room, which is something they had never done before.

A POLTERGEIST IS PRESENT

It was not long after the haunting began that the girls also started to experience poltergeist activity. In Stacie's room she has a collection of bobblehead figures that sit on a shelf along the wall. The bobbleheads always face out, but Stacie began to find that they would all be facing the wall, although the other roommates swore they had nothing to do with it. The girls also started finding chairs stacked on the kitchen table for no apparent reason, and then a few weeks later Kristin had an unnerving experience while the other two girls were back home visiting their families during spring break.

Kristin had heard some strange noises coming from Linsay's room, so she walked down the hall to investigate. When she entered Linsay's room she discovered all of the dresser drawers had been pulled out and all of the clothes were thrown on the floor in the middle of the room. In addition, a blanket had been thrown over the computer, the corner of Linsay's bed had been moved out a few inches, and her graduation gown was hanging on a coat hanger from the ceiling fan. All three girls were in their last year of school and were only weeks from graduating. Were these spirits trying to tell the girls they were ready for them to graduate and leave by hanging Linsay's gown from the fan?

Later that same night Kristin began to hear the distinct sound of an old woman singing coming from Stacie's room. She was actually able to capture the singing on a recording using her iPhone,® as the singing continued for a few hours. Disturbed by the experiences she was having, Kristin sprinkled sea salt in front of the door of her room for protection. As soon as she did she started to hear a loud knocking on the door to her room. Her door was slightly ajar, and she could see through the crack in the door that a shadow person was pacing back and forth outside her doorway, knocking repeatedly in frustration and trying to enter the room. Apparently the salt barrier had worked and this spirit was quite angry about it. A few minutes later Kristin heard a loud rapping on the walls going around her room. It sounded like fingers impatiently tapping on the walls all around her.

In a panic Kristin called her father Scott and told him what was happening in the house. Fearing that Kristin was alone in the home with this activity going on Scott called Kristin's brother, who lived nearby in Savannah, and asked him to go by the house and check on his sister. When her brother arrived the singing was still going on in Stacie's room. The two siblings then sat down in the living room to discuss what Kristin had been experiencing. The two of them were seated on the couch, talking for a few minutes, when they suddenly noticed a chair from the dining room table was now sitting beside the couch. Neither of them had seen the chair move, but it had somehow moved by itself. It was as if someone had pulled up a chair to join in the conversation they were having.

THE ENTITY IN THE CLOSET RETURNS

Soon after returning from spring break Linsay began to see the dark figure in her room again. This figure would watch her as she lay in bed, trying to sleep. Linsay would pull the covers over her head and then look back out from under her blanket, and on many occasions he would still be standing there, glaring at her. The girls had already been experiencing the feeling of being watched when no one else was around, but now these entities in the home were making themselves known by showing their true form. It was no wonder there was such an urgency in Scott's voice when I had spoken with him on the phone that afternoon. We decided to set up an investigation of the home two nights later and Scott came down from New York to participate.

A TERRIFYING WARNING

The morning after Scott arrived at the house he decided to take a quick shower. Upon stepping out of the shower he noticed that a chilling message had been written on the mirror, yet the bathroom door was still locked and he was the only one in the room. Scrawled across the mirror were the words, "They are mine." The entities in the home evidently knew the reason for Scott's arrival and they were not willing to give up too easily. While Scott was at the house preparing for that night's investigation Kim and I were running around town, picking up holy water from the Cathedral of John the Baptist to bless the house with. When we arrived later that night there was an ominous feeling as soon as we set foot in the home. Although the neighborhood was quite lively when we pulled up, as soon as we entered the home there was a strange silence all around, as if someone had draped a large blanket over the entire house.

Throughout most of the investigation the place remained eerily calm, with very little activity at all. A few hours after we began we did have an unnerving experience in Linsay's room. We were all seated in the middle of the room, conducting an EVP session, when our K2 EMF meter began to go off repeatedly, spiking higher and higher each time. Linsay then asked: "Were you the one that was in my room?" A male entity then clearly replied, "While you were sleeping." This was apparently the same spirit that came out of her closet almost every single night to torment her. At the same time the whole room began to fill with the strong scent of cheap cologne. It smelled like Musk or English Leather, and the smell had come from out of thin air. Thankfully a few moments after the strange smell had appeared it quickly dissipated. We caught a few other pieces of audio that night, but it seemed that these entities were toying with us and had no desire to show us their full power.

After completing the investigation Kim and I did a full blessing on the home, including prayers, holy water, smudging with sage, and a few other methods. After finishing the blessing the house felt much more inviting. There was not the heavy, foreboding feeling that was present there before and the overall atmosphere was much lighter. The blessing at first seemed to work, because for almost two weeks the girls did not experience any paranormal activity in the house. Then one night, just as the girls were starting to get comfortable again, the presence returned, and this time it was angry.

Kristin was lying in bed asleep when she felt someone was standing over her. She then heard the sound of a mirror break in her room. The mirror sat on a dresser on the other side of the room and there was no explanation as to what could have broken it. All of a sudden Kristin began to feel scratches all over her arms and legs, and then she noticed there was broken mirror glass all over her bed. Whatever had caused the scratches had used the mirror glass to perform its task. These scratches were in groups of threes, a tell tale sign of demonic activity. Many scratch marks in demonic cases appear in groups of threes, which is a way of mocking the Holy Trinity. Horrified beyond belief Kristin called her father, who then told all three girls to leave the house immediately and go to a hotel. As the girls were in the car and leaving the house they noticed that someone or something must have been standing in the front window, watching the girls leave. As they were backing down the driveway they noticed a light turn on in that room and something opened the blinds, as if watching them leave the house. The blinds were then shut and the light in that room turned off.

A PRIEST IS CALLED

As soon as he had gotten off the phone with Kristen, Scott gave me a call. This case was now beyond my hands, and we both agreed that clergy needed to get involved immediately. I contacted a Catholic priest who happened to be the vicar general of the Diocese of Savannah at the Cathedral of St. John the Baptist to come out and do an exorcism on the home, and he agreed that this was indeed necessary. The only problem was he was leaving for a nine-day conference the following afternoon and he would not be able to tend to the case until he returned. But after reviewing the case file, which also included photos of Kristin's recent attack, he said: "Tell the girls to be ready; we are going to do this first thing in the morning. I need to do this before my trip; this can't wait another nine days."

After the exorcism the home stayed quiet, and there was only one other strange occurrence that happened right before the three girls graduated and moved out. About a week before they left Kristin was packing and left a box on the couch in the living room. As she came out of her room she noticed there was a woman sitting on the couch with her hand in the box, looking back at her and smiling. The woman looked to be in her mid- to late thirties, and she looked like she was strung out on drugs. A few seconds afterward the woman vanished. Was this perhaps the spirit of someone who may have overdosed and died in the house during its vacant years? We may never know, but apparently this entity was happy to see the girls were moving out.

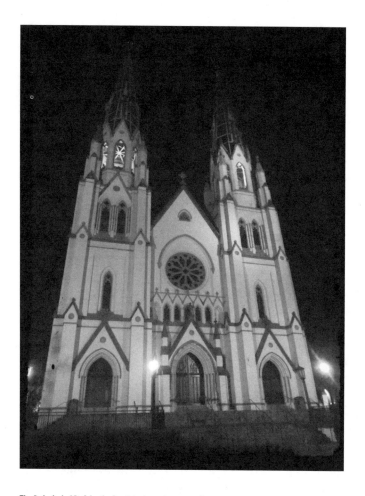

The Cathedral of St. John the Baptist, whose vicar general performed the exorcism on Kristin Haglund's home.

THE BEINGS RETURN

Not long after the girls moved out of the house two other young college students moved in and signed a year lease. In less than a month these students broke their lease and moved out of the house. Evidently one of them had been picked up and thrown across the room by an unseen force, leaving a large bruised handprint in the middle of his back. Apparently these entities are not only tied to this house, though, because Linsay is still having experiences, even though she has since moved back home to Charlotte, North Carolina. One recent afternoon she was out for a jog and she had on headphones, listening to music. After a few minutes her music quit playing and a loud crackling began to come through the speakers.

A deep male voice then clearly came through and said, "I've found you," and then the music started to play again.

A few months after the case I received a telephone call from the producers of the Syfy Channel's show, *Paranormal Witness*. They were interested in hearing about some of our most disturbing recent cases, and of course this case was the first one that came to mind. After speaking with Scott and the girls they agreed to appear on the show and tell their story. The episode aired on season 5, episode 2 in August 2016, and it was entitled "They Are Mine," based on what Scott had seen written in the bathroom mirror that fateful morning in his daughter's home. Unfortunately the show left out quite a few important elements of the case, including the investigation and the exorcism. In addition they took a few liberties with the story itself. Not long after the story aired, *Paranormal Witness* decided to publish a follow-up article to the case on their website for which I was interviewed that added in the missing elements to the story.

This case remains the most horrifying encounter with negative entities I have ever experienced. Throughout the entire case my family was also experiencing activity in our home. It really took a toll on our whole family, including my two daughters. Needless to say, I am glad we were able to help out where we could, and that the girls were able to have some solace. These demonic hauntings can be very aggressive, and on many occasions they can come back even after multiple blessings and exorcisms. To this day I remain great friends with Scott Haglund and his family, and every time they are in town we always meet up for a late night dinner and a few drinks. Should you ever encounter what you believe to be the onset of a demonic encounter do not attempt to rectify the situation yourself; your best bet in this type of situation is to call a priest.

CHAPTER 18

A FATAL FALL

The Sorrel-Weed House Investigation

The Sorrel-Weed house was built in 1839, and completed in 1840, for Francis Sorrel, who had the home built for his second wife, Matilda, as a wedding present.

I believe that almost every paranormal investigator worth their salt has their own wish list of locations they would love to investigate, and I am no different. The Sorrel-Weed House had been near the top of my list of haunted Savannah locations to investigate for quite a while, and it was five years after I began paranormal research that I was finally allowed overnight access to the property. A few years before I moved to this grand old city I had first seen the Sorrel-Weed house on the Syfy Channel when the Atlantic Paranormal Society (TAPS) crew from the hit television show *Ghost Hunters* investigated the place. It had first aired as their Halloween special on October 31, 2005, as the fourteenth episode of the second season. I was amazed at the evidence they were able to capture, including one very clear EVP captured in the carriage house of a woman screaming: "Help, stop!! Stop it!! Oh my God! Oh my God!"

The Travel Channel's *Ghost Adventures* crew was there investigating in 2014, which later aired in May of that year in their "Haunted Savannah" episode (Season 9, Episode 10). Both teams were able to capture some amazing evidence during their investigations there, so as you can imagine I was thrilled when I received an email from Orlin Reynolds, the director of the home, saying he would allow us overnight access to investigate the place. With all of the tragic past surrounding the home's history I was very optimistic about the outcome of our investigation even before I delved into the home's dark beginnings.

THE BRITISH LINE OF DEFENSE

Although the home has a lot of history tied to it, seeds for the hauntings surrounding the building were planted much earlier, many years before the home was ever built. The property where the Sorrel-Weed House now sits was once part of the center point of the front line of a Revolutionary War-era British defense fort. The British had captured the colony of Savannah on December 29, 1778, and by 1779, they had built forts surrounding the colony, one of which was Spring Hill Redoubt, the site of the famous Siege of Savannah battle. The fort on the front line of defense sat in what is now Madison Square, as well as on part of the lot on which the Sorrel-Weed House now sits. Prior to the Siege of Savannah French and American forces had attacked this fort with cannon fire, and this house now sits over part of that historic site.

HISTORY OF THE HOME

The Sorrel-Weed House, which sits at 6 West Harris Street on the north end of Madison Square, was built in 1839, for a wealthy shipping merchant named Francis Sorrel. Francis had this home built as a wedding present for his second wife, Matilda. Constructed by noted architect Charles Cluskey, this home is one of the most significant examples of Greek Revival architecture in the downtown area. Francis lost his first wife, Lucinda, twelve years earlier in 1827 to yellow fever. He then married Lucinda's younger sister, Matilda Sorrel, a few years later. He had three children by Lucinda before her passing, then went on to have eight more children by her sister Matilda, of which only five survived to adulthood. Two of Matilda's children died as infants, and she lost one child at only six years of age. Among his most well-known offspring was his son, Gilbert Moxley Sorrel, who became a well-decorated brigadier general in the Confederacy, as well as his son, Francis Sorrel Jr., who later became a Princeton graduate and a well-respected physician.

Francis Sorrel's story begins much earlier in his native land Santo Domingo, in the Dominican Republic. He was originally born Mathurin-François Sorrel in the Miragoane Parish of Petit Goâve in 1793, and he later changed his name to Francis upon moving to the United States. He was considered a quadroon—one-quarter African American—and was one of the *gens de couleur libres*, or free people of color. As a young child Francis was saved by a trusted slave from a massacre by white colonists that occurred during a massive slave revolt. After seeing the horrors of slavery in his homeland Francis still managed to become one of Savannah's wealthiest businessmen with his own slaves. How after seeing the atrocities of this despicable act was he able to participate in the practice himself? All the while his fellow comrades in Savannah's upper crust of society had no idea that Mr. Sorrel was indeed one-quarter African American. The Sorrels continued to thrive in the opulence of Savannah's elite for many years, and they were known to host the best soirées in town. Francis Sorrel Jr. later went on to practice medicine in the home, with his offices in the bottom floor of the property.

To accommodate for his growing family, Francis Sorrel Sr. had a home built right next door to the house at 12 West Harris Street in 1856. In 1859, Mr. Sorrel sold his home at 6 West Harris Street to a Mr. Henry D. Weed. Francis then later moved next door into the home at 12 West Harris Street. There are conflicting stories as to whether Francis and his family immediately moved into the home at 12 West Harris Street, or if they remained a few years at 6 West Harris before moving next door. We do know that Gen. Robert E. Lee visited Francis at the Sorrel-Weed mansion in fall 1861 and spring 1862, indicating that perhaps the Sorrels were still in the home at that time.

A FALL FROM GRACE

On March 27, 1860, tragedy once again struck Francis Sorrel, as he lost his second wife Matilda to suicide. Family papers suggest Matilda had been suffering from depression for quite a while and she had not been in the best mental state. Perhaps she was grief-stricken over the loss of her three children over the years, or maybe it was something else entirely. Regardless of the reason, she had jumped from a balcony window and into the garden courtyard below, where she was instantly killed. Discrepancies suggest if Francis and his family were living next door at 12 West Harris Street at the time of Matilda's death, then she would have committed suicide in a home other than the Sorrel-Weed House; she would have then died next door. Regardless, in those days both homes shared the same courtyard, so either way she would have been found dead in approximately the same location.

MOLLY'S TALE

Another very popular tale suggests that Mr. Sorrel had been having an affair with one of his slaves, a young Haitian girl named Molly. Francis had quickly bestowed his affections upon this young girl, and having been from the same native island as he the two had quite a bit in common. It is believed Matilda uncovered the details of her husband's illustrious affair and committed suicide in a fit of despair. Molly was found dead a few weeks later in the second floor of the carriage house, hanging by a noose from the rafters in what would have then been her quarters. Theories suggest that perhaps Francis, distraught over the loss of his wife, murdered Molly in cold blood. Others surmise that Francis's other slaves murdered Molly out of anger when they heard about the affair. Even more likely Molly may have committed suicide, upset over the outcome of her affair with Francis.

After looking over records at the Georgia Historical Society, as well as other sources, I could find no evidence to show that Molly existed. I will say that records of the slave trade in Savannah, as well as records of who owned which slaves, are very sparse. We have records of almost anything you need, but when it comes to evidence of slavery many records appear to have been destroyed over the years, and those that are accessible do not tell much. The story of Molly could very well have happened, but it also seems there would have been some documentation in Savannah's newspapers detailing at least Molly's suicide/murder. We may never know for sure whether or not the Molly story happened, but with that said, the room in the carriage house on the second floor known as "Molly's Room" is still one of the most haunted areas on the property.

Did Molly really die in that room she continues to haunt, waiting for someone to finally hear her side of the story, or has this been a yarn spun over the years to add to the hauntings of the home? Moreover, where did the story come from? When I first interviewed Orlin Reynolds he went on to explain that, "Molly's story was passed down to us from the Weed family to Abram J. Cohen, who then passed the story on to us." In addition, several psychic mediums have described the same grisly encounter in detail and claim that Molly was indeed murdered there. Details surrounding this supposed scandal may never be uncovered, but there is definitely more than one reason why the Sorrel-Weed House has gained notoriety as one of the most haunted houses in the United States—and it has rightfully earned that rank.

Francis Sorrel passed away on May 5, 1870, just ten years after he lost his second wife, Matilda. Henry Weed continued to live at 6 West Harris Street with his family until the late 1880s. By 1889, his son, Joseph Weed, is listed as living in the home with his wife, Sarah. Joseph was the owner of the J. D. Weed Company, as well as president of the Savannah Bank & Trust Company. By 1907, Sarah Weed was a widow, and continued to live in the home with her daughter, Josephine Weed, until 1915. The home remained vacant for a few years; then, in 1934, Jack E. Brantley and his wife Laura moved into the property and opened their antique shop, Brantley Studio.

⨀ A GRISLY DISCOVERY

Throughout the next few years various tenants came and went until 1941, when Abraham J. Cohen purchased the building. In 1946, his son, Abraham J. Cohen Jr., and his wife Gloria occupied the home. Shortly after acquiring the property the two opened the Lady Jane Dress Shop in the downstairs of the old house while maintaining living quarters on the upper floors. The dress shop and its owners occupied the property until 1996, when Stephen Bader purchased the house and began renovations. In 2005, he opened it up to historic tours of the property, as well as night time ghost tours. During renovations in the bottom floor of the home in 1996, the concrete flooring was removed to restore the property to its originality. Upon excavating the area beneath the floor, after only a few shovelfuls of dirt there was an amazing discovery. Many artifacts were unearthed, including human bones, musket balls, bayonet parts, cannon balls, and parts of British uniforms. These were believed to remain from the center point of the front line of the British defense fort at which the Sorrel-Weed House now sits on a portion.

THE HAUNTINGS

Orlin Reynolds, the house tour director of the home, has worked there for many years, and although he likes to look at everything from a skeptic's stand point, he has had quite a few encounters in the home that could not easily be explained. Even the owner of the home, Steve Bader, had numerous experiences when he first purchased the property. When he first moved into the house he would hear strange sounds coming from the downstairs parlors as he lay upstairs asleep. It would sound as if a party were going on downstairs, with the sounds of music and singing, as well as raucous laughter and the chiming of crystal. It seemed the elegant parties the Sorrels were known for still continued to this day.

One late evening, as Orlin was closing up, he heard a rustling sound coming from the family dining room. It sounded like a light clothing material, almost like a jacket or duffel bag type of material rustling together; maybe even the rustling of taffeta. Then all of a sudden he heard someone run down the stairs that lead to the basement. Thinking perhaps a tour guest had decided to hide out and explore the building, or even worse, that a burglar had entered the home, Orlin grabbed a large stick and searched the entire basement, but no one was there. All of the basement doors were dead-bolted and the only way out was the way Orlin had just come from.

Many patrons of the Sorrel-Weed House ghost tour have had their own brush with the afterlife. On occasions too many to count, there have been apparitions captured in photographs of ladies in period dress and soldiers in uniform in the twin parlors on the main floor. Yet there are others who have witnessed a dark shadow figure peeking out of Molly's room into the upstairs carriage house living area. Other sightings have been of a small, little girl who has been known to appear in the library of the home, quite possibly the spirit of one of Matilda's children she lost. Even the staff and tour guides report paranormal incidents on a regular basis. One evening, a tour guide was standing downstairs when all of a sudden she saw a lady in a long dress standing outside the door to the family dining area. The woman then turned and ran into the room very fast. When the guide went and looked into the room it was completely empty.

It would seem the Sorrel-Weed House has its fair share of ghosts, but perhaps the most disturbing entity that haunts the property is the ghost of Matilda Sorrel. Her spirit has been seen in the courtyard, as well as in the outside window looking into the ladies' parlor. She is always seen wearing a long black antebellum dress, and at first most folks that see her assume she is a real person until she disappears a few moments later. She is consistently seen as angry or in mourning, possibly over either her husband's affair or over the depression that led to her suicide.

THE INVESTIGATION

I arrived at the Sorrel-Weed House one warm night in late April 2015 to conduct our investigation with Gwen Kersten, Kristina Kersten, and David Jackson. Our equipment technician and photographer Kris Kersten was in Alaska, and we had trouble getting a sitter that night, so my wife Kim could not be there. I had worked with Kris's mother, Gwen, and his sister Kristina on a few cases before, and Gwen has done a lot of work to support our research over the years. David was interested in becoming one of our tour guides so I wanted to have him there so he could see how our investigations worked first hand. As soon as we arrived we were met by Orlin, who already had some interesting news to share with us. Evidently a few hours before our team had arrived for the investigation one of the tour guides had mentioned to Orlin he had heard someone in the carriage house cussing in French as he was going up the stairs. We had not even walked in the door and the home seemed to be waiting for us to arrive, as if it were beckoning us to enter its halls.

We decided to split up into two teams, with David and I taking the main house first and Gwen and Kristina investigating the carriage house. Within just a few minutes of arriving in Molly's room Gwen's recorder captured a chilling EVP of a female voice that appeared to be humming. Neither Gwen nor Kristina had heard the sound on location, but upon playing the recording back there was no doubt as to what they had just captured. Was this the ghost of Molly or Matilda? Or had they encountered an entirely different spirit all together? Later in the evening, in that same room, I caught a rather unnerving EVP. I had just said: "It's okay to talk to us, you aren't going to be in any trouble." A few seconds later there was a very clear spirit response, "Yeah we will."

In addition to all of the evidence we captured in Molly's room of the carriage house, the bottom floor of the home was also quite active. Toward the end of the night the whole team was in the room the staff likes to call the "surgery room." This is where Dr. Francis Sorrel Jr. ran his physician's office and is one of the most haunted rooms in the house. All four of us were seated in the center of the room conducting an EVP session and the place began to feel very heavy and dense. A moment later my audio recorder caught the voice of a male spirit that said, "Let us go." Maybe these spirits were ready for us to go and leave them alone, but we could also surmise that there was a darker entity preventing these others from coming forward, which could also explain the "Yeah we will" response when we told them they would not get into trouble for communicating with us. We gave the investigation a while longer, but after these last few EVPs not much else happened. I was very pleased with how successful the night had gone and even more excited about what we were able to capture.

The Sorrel-Weed House has been ranked by many as one of the top ten most haunted places in the United States; it was also featured on the *Most Terrifying Places in America* television show in 2010, among numerous other national accolades. They conduct daytime history tours and nighttime ghost tours seven days a week, and the staff and patrons still report ghostly encounters all the time. The night time tours also include the use of ghost hunting equipment, and guests regularly catch EVPs, photos of apparitions, and other phenomena. In fact, about a month before our investigation of the home a man was scratched while on the tour by an unseen entity. Unfortunately Orlin Reynolds left in December 2015 to pursue other interests, but the home still remains open to the public. If you decide you are brave enough to do the tour, make sure you keep your recorders rolling and your cameras ready, or you may just miss your opportunity to communicate with the other side.

CHAPTER 19

NO REST FOR THE WICKED

The Old Chatham County Jail
Investigation

The Old Chatham County Jail housed Savannah's most notorious criminals before its closing.

In the beginning of 2015, I began writing the book you are reading now. I was going through all of my case files and interviews from my investigation at B&D Burgers on Congress Street and I had a few questions I needed to ask Gena Bilbo, the restaurant's old marketing manager. When I gave her a call she mentioned she would be glad to help with the story in any way she could, but that she was now working for the Chatham County Sheriff's Department as their director of public affairs. After we finished talking about the B&D case, Gena mentioned that for Halloween this year the sheriff's department was going to be conducting a haunted house fundraiser at the Old Chatham County Jail on Montgomery Street, which had been vacant of inmates ever since 1989. They were going to be raising money for the Wounded Warrior Project, as well as two other local charities: Explorer Post 876 and the Chatham County Youth Commission.

Whenever there is a chance we can do some good with our research, especially with charitable organizations, we are always willing to help. According to Gena, although they were going to fabricate the haunted house as an attraction, the building was evidently actually haunted! They were interested in having our team come out to investigate the property to authenticate the hauntings that were occurring there prior to the haunted house opening. Over the years we have investigated some pretty disturbing places, including hospitals, sanitariums, and the like, but this was to be our first investigation of a jail, and I had no idea it would turn out to be one of the most successful investigations we have ever conducted.

THE HISTORY

The Old Chatham County Jail is at 145 Montgomery Street in the Historic District of Savannah and sits directly beside the Chatham County Courthouse. Many years before the jail was constructed there was a small, wooden framed house that sat on the lot. This home was built in 1885, for an old widow and dressmaker named Mrs. Isabella Robinson. She lived there with another widow, a seamstress named Miss Lottie Lewis. The two women lived in the home and operated their small dress shop from the building for over a decade. By 1897, both women had died, and there is no listing of any structure on the lot for quite a few years, leading us to believe it remained vacant for a long while. In 1940, Helmey's Garage occupied the lot and is listed in the city directories as being at 145 Montgomery Street. Helmey's was owned and operated by a Mr. Sherman I. Helmey and his wife Louise. By 1949, the lot was once again empty and remained vacant until 1974.

In 1974, the City of Savannah had the Chatham County Jail constructed at 145 Montgomery Street, right next door to the Chatham County Courthouse. By 1976, the jail began housing inmates, and continued to remain in operation until 1989, when the building was finally vacated and all of the inmates were moved to a new facility. Since that time the building has remained mostly unoccupied, except for a short while in which it was used to house archives. For thirteen unlucky years the jail housed Savannah's most hardened criminals, many of them murderers, rapists, and other violent offenders awaiting trial. During interviews Brian Counihan and Russell Smith, both former guards at the jail, reported numerous deaths. There were fights, shankings, and even inmates found dead from suicide by hanging themselves with their bed sheets. Deputy Smith went on to state that, "This was not the same direct supervision that you see in jails today. Things were a lot rougher back then."

THE ALDAY MURDERS

One of the most notorious criminals to ever walk these halls was Carl Isaacs, orchestrator of the infamous Alday Family murders. For almost a year Isaacs was housed on the third floor in isolation awaiting trial. Brian Counihan still remembers his first encounter with Issacs:

> The first day that I ever worked this floor [the third floor] I came on shift and as I walked by his cell he said, "Officer Counihan," trying to get my attention. The thing was, we had stopped wearing name tags months before Isaacs arrived, so I still have not figured out how he knew my name. Isaacs was an eerie fellow, a very evil individual.

On May 5, 1973, petty criminal Carl Isaacs, Wayne Coleman, and George Dundee escaped from the Maryland State Prison. Along the way they picked up Carl's brother, Billy Isaacs, and went on a crime spree that resulted in multiple deaths before they were apprehended less than two weeks later. A few days after escaping the four men were in McConnellsburg, Pennsylvania, when all of a sudden the white pickup truck they had recently stolen began to have trouble. The men were pulled off to the side of the road when a young high school student named Richard Wayne Miller came driving past. Miller recognized the truck as belonging to a friend of his and he quickly approached the men, demanding they return the truck to its rightful owner immediately. The men responded by pulling a gun on Miller and forcing him into his own vehicle to drive them all out of state.

By the time Miller and the men reached Maryland they asked him to pull over, where they then led him to a small wooded area and murdered him. The gang had decided to make a break for Mexico, but four days later, while in the rural town Donalsonville, Georgia, in southwest Seminole County, things took a turn for the worse. The four men were looking for gas, money, and weapons, and on the afternoon of May 14, 1973, they found themselves driving down a desolate dirt road toward the Alday Family Farm. There they brutally murdered Jerry Alday, as well as his two brothers, Chester and Jimmy. All three men were found dead in the two bedrooms of the home, along with Jerry's father, Ned Alday, and his brother, Aubrey. All five men had been shot to death by Isaacs and his crew.

Sadly enough, the brutality did not end there. Two days after the bodies of the five Alday men were discovered the body of Jerry's wife, Mary Alday, was found in the woods near the home. She had been raped repeatedly before being mercilessly shot to death. Carl Isaacs was later convicted of murder and was put to death by lethal injection in 2003. His brother, Billy Isaacs, served twenty years in prison and later died a free man in 2009. George Dundee died in prison in 2006, and Wayne Coleman, the last of the Alday family killers, is still serving a life sentence at the Georgia State Prison in Reidsville. The horrors of the Alday Family murders were the second largest mass murder in Georgia history, and even now the echoes from that tragic event reverberate through Seminole County, Georgia.

When the Chatham County Sheriff's Department decided to start converting the old jail into a haunted house strange things began to occur in the building. Cory Harper, who works for the Sheriff's Department, was in charge of putting together the attraction, so he spent quite a bit of time alone in the place. One afternoon, not long after starting renovations on the old jail, Cory and a coworker were walking down the third floor hallway. Out of nowhere a heavy metal panel went flying off the wall and crashed into the other side of the hallway, as if propelled by some unseen force. This panel had been secured to the wall and it weighed at least 150 pounds. It would have taken some serious strength for it to go as far, and as fast, as it did all by itself. After speaking with Brian Counihan and Russell Smith about their experiences while working in the jail it seemed the hauntings had been happening here for quite a while. As Russell described:

> You would hear strange noises quite often; you would hear doors close when no one else was around and the inmates were all locked in their cells. Sometimes you could feel an unexplained cold, yet nothing would be around to explain the cause of it. There was always that feeling that something was around, yet nobody else would be there; just strange, eerie feelings.

"You would even hear strange noises in the hallways near the stairwells, but then you would walk down the hall and nothing would be there," added Counihan. Even Gena went on to say that she did not like being by herself in the building. "It always feels like someone is watching me," she said.

I knew that with Gena's wizardry in marketing there was most likely going to be some media when we arrived for our investigation in mid-September 2015, but I had no idea how much press she had contacted about the event. When I arrived with Kim and Kris that night I was greeted by Cory, who was going to be staying with us throughout the investigation, as well as members of several other media outlets. We were also joined by WTOC News here in Savannah, as well as Karson Hoagland of the *Savannah Morning News* and Russ Matthess, a journalist for www.designingfear. com. Once again Gena had outdone herself.

THE INVESTIGATION

As soon as we arrived I was rushing to set up our DVR system; with eight cameras and hundreds of feet of cable to run through all four floors of the jail it was going to take quite a while. As soon as we had started setting up Kim began turning on audio recorders. While everyone was outside the building grabbing equipment one of the recorders in the third floor hallway captured our first EVP of the night; a clear voice of a male spirit said, "Bout time they got here." Evidently these spirits knew we were coming and they were ready to communicate. It is not surprising, considering this property remained vacant for years and this malevolent energy had just been sitting inside, festering and growing, until it had recently started to make itself known to the staff.

We headed first into the basement to try a few EVP sessions. Evidently there has been a rumor for years that there is a tunnel that leads from the old jail into the basement of the courthouse that they used to transport prisoners back and forth from trial. According to Cory this was no rumor, and we decided to head first into that tunnel to try and capture some evidence. On the way down to the basement we took the old elevator, which in itself was creepy enough. Before we could step foot off the elevator and into the basement hallway Kim's audio recorder caught an EVP that said, "Get the fuck out of here." These spirits were aggressive and not all of them seemed happy with our presence here.

A little while later, while in the third floor hallway, Kim's recorder caught another Class A EVP, this time of a spirit that growled, "Kidnap and hurt them!" It was now apparent that some of these spirits intended to do us harm. In the third floor medical office, where all inmates were pronounced dead by a medical examiner if there was indeed a death in the jail, another chilling EVP was caught. This time it sounded as if two spirits were communicating with each other. One of them said, "I'm about to get her good," and the other one then replied, "I know." We think that these entities were referring to them trying to hurt Kim, as she was the only female in the room at the time that this audio evidence was captured. Throughout the investigation we caught fifty EVPs, and most of them were Class A, which is more audio evidence than we have captured on any other case. Although we captured a lot of EVPs throughout the entire building, the majority of our evidence was captured on the third floor. This makes sense, because this is where they housed mental health inmates in one wing and isolation inmates in the other—where all of the murderers and the more violent criminals were incarcerated.

A THERMAL IMAGE IS CAPTURED

A few hours into the investigation we had an unnerving encounter with a very tall, dark shadow figure. Cory had been using our FLIR thermal imaging camera to scan through the building, looking for anomalies in temperature. At one point he started seeing this shadow figure walking around in the kitchen on the second floor, right between he and Kim. He snapped a still image of the figure crouched by a wall. Just a few minutes later we were all in a common room right outside the cells on the third floor and I was seated Indian style in the room, asking EVP questions. All of a sudden Cory could see the shadow figure pacing back and forth right outside the hall. This figure was over six feet tall, and it turned around in the hallway and came right though the door and into the room we were in. The figure was much taller than the doorway, yet it did not duck down to enter the room; it simply walked right through the top of the wall that was above the door. Cory managed to snap a quick thermal image of it, and this thing was enormous! After Cory snapped the image the entity quickly retreated from the room and returned down the hall where it continued to pace in anticipation.

Although inmates could glimpse the outside from the ceiling, the rec room was by far the most depressing room in the entire jail.

There was one room in the jail throughout the entire investigation that seemed to get to everyone that was there that night. This was probably the most unassuming of all the uncomfortable areas in the jail, because it was the third floor recreation room. This was a concrete walled room with no ceiling above, so one could look out into the open air. The ceiling was covered in rusted fencing and razor wire to deter any inmate from the idea of escaping. Here inmates were allowed one hour per day to exercise or play basketball. The room was overwhelmingly depressing and the air was heavy and thick with sorrow—so thick you could spread it on toast. It may seem that being incarcerated behind bars in a cell twenty-three hours a day may have been bad, but this seemed a far worse punishment. You could see the sky, sun, and clouds, and even smell the air if the wind was just right, but this was all just a tease. The feeling of what it was like to be incarcerated really hit home when we walked out into the recreation yard and realized this was supposed to be a privilege. This was the one area where Kim, who is very empathic, had trouble staying for too long due to the overwhelming flow of sadness that was all around.

Our investigation of the Old Chatham County Jail was a huge success, and thanks to Gena and her marketing prowess, the story aired multiple times on WTOC News, WSAV News, WJCL-ABC News, WTGS-FOX News 28, in the *Savannah Morning News*, in multiple articles by Russ Matthess with www.designingfear.com, and through Georgia Public Broadcasting. The haunted house fund raiser raised over $50,000 collectively for all three charities and it was a huge success. I suggest that if you want to see the old jail while you are visiting Savannah be sure to stop by and take a picture of it, because the city will be tearing down the old building soon and perhaps these troubled spirits will finally get some rest.

In December 2016, I was approached by Rob Saffi, producer of Destination America's hit television show *Paranormal Lockdown*, which stars Nick Groff (previously of the *Ghost Adventures* show) and Katrina Weidman (previously of the show *Paranormal State*). We filmed a few days later and the show aired in March 2017, as the season two finale. During Nick and Katrina's investigation of the jail they were able to capture evidence of the same shadow figure we encountered during our investigation.

HOW TO GET INVOLVED

The Wounded Warrior Project is a charity and military veterans organization that assists wounded veterans who have been injured while serving our country in battle. To get involved contact www.woundedwarriorproject.org.

Pictured left to right are Nick Groff, Ryan Dunn, and Katrina Weidman during the filming of *Paranormal Lockdown*.

Explorer Post 876 is a charity organization that assists young men and women who are interested in employment in the law enforcement field through mentoring, motivating, and preparing these individuals for a successful career. To get involved contact Explorer Post 876 at the Chatham County Sheriff's Office, phone (912) 651-3743.

The Chatham County Youth Commission is an organization that prepares local youth for leadership roles in the community and helps to get them involved in government. To get involved contact the Chatham County Youth Commission:

124 Bull Street, Suite 110
Savannah, GA 31401
(912) 652-7964
email: youthcommission@chathamcounty.org

AFTERWORD

The Savannah Ghost Research Society at their investigation of Bobby Mackey's in Wilder, Kentucky (left to right): former investigator Shaun Holcomb, Ryan Dunn, and Kris Kersten.

My paranormal research team has been investigating the paranormal for many years and we still regularly take on new cases. We have dealt with all manner of hauntings, including poltergeists, shadow people, malevolent spirits, and demonic entities. Should you find yourself in a situation where you are in need of our services, please feel free to contact us at (912) 665-8886, on Facebook at Savannah Ghost Research Society, or you can email us at savannahghostresearchsociety@gmail.com. We would be more than happy to help you in any way we can.

If you would like to hear the paranormal evidence mentioned in this book and you are in the Savannah area, we would love to have you on our tour, *Afterlife Tours*, which features real paranormal evidence at every stop captured by our research team. We conduct tours Monday through Saturday at 8:00 p.m. and 10:00 p.m. and are closed on Sundays. You can purchase tickets either by calling us at (912) 398-7820, by visiting our website at www.afterlifetours.net, or by emailing us at afterlifetours@yahoo.com. We also regularly perform public investigations at the Moon River Brewery, so be sure to ask about our upcoming investigation schedule. Thank you for taking the time to read this book, and I hope that you enjoyed reading it as much as I enjoyed writing it.

We are always here and we are always available.

VISITOR AND CONTACT INFORMATION

for the Haunted Locations Mentioned in this Book

ALLIGATOR SOUL RESTAURANT
114 Barnard Street
Savannah, GA 31401
Hours of Operation:
Open daily from 5:30 p.m. to 10-ish

THE BALLASTONE INN
14 East Oglethorpe Avenue
Savannah, GA 31401
(912) 236-1484
www.ballastone.com

B&D BURGERS ON CONGRESS STREET
209 West Congress Street
Savannah, GA 31401
www.bdburgers.net
Hours of Operation:
Sunday to Thursday 11 a.m. to 12 a.m.
Friday and Saturday 11 a.m. to 2 a.m.

CHURCHILL'S PUB
13 West Bay Street
Savannah, GA 31401
(912) 232-8501
www.thebritishpub.com
Hours of Operation:
Sunday to Thursday 5 p.m. to 1:00 a.m.
Friday and Saturday 5 p.m. to 2:00 a.m.

THE CONGRESS STREET SOCIAL CLUB
411 West Congress Street
Savannah, GA 31401
(912) 238-1985
www.congressstreetsocialclub.com
Hours of Operation:
Monday to Saturday 12 p.m. to 3 a.m.
Sunday 12:30 p.m. to 2 a.m.

THE CRYSTAL BEER PARLOR
301 West Jones Street
Savannah, GA 31401
(912) 349-1000
www.crystalbeerparlor.com
Hours of Operation:
Sunday to Thursday 11 a.m. to 10 p.m.
Friday and Saturday 11 a.m. to 11 p.m.

THE GEORGIA STATE RAILROAD MUSEUM
655 Louisville Road
Savannah, GA 31401
www.chsgeorgia.org/Railroad-Museum.html
Hours of Operation:
Monday to Sunday 9 a.m. to 5 p.m.
Admission:
$10 per adult
$6 per child (ages 2–12)

THE HAMILTON-TURNER INN
330 Abercorn Street
Savannah, GA 31401
(912) 233-1833
www.hamilton-turnerinn.com

JUAREZ RESTAURANT
420 East Broughton Street
Savannah, GA 31401
(The Juarez Restaurant is permanently
closed)

KEVIN BARRY'S IRISH PUB
117 West River Street
Savannah, GA 31401
(912) 233-9626
www.kevinbarrys.com
Hours of Operation:
Monday to Saturday 11 a.m. to 3 a.m.
Sunday 12:30 p.m. to 2 a.m.
(Live Irish music nightly)

THE MARSHALL HOUSE HOTEL
123 East Broughton Street
Savannah, GA 31401
(912) 644-7896
www.marshallhouse.com

THE OLD CHATHAM COUNTY JAIL
145 Montgomery Street
Savannah, GA 31401

OLD FORT JACKSON
1 Fort Jackson Road
Savannah, GA, 31404
(912) 232-3945
www.chsgeorgia.org/Old-Fort-Jackson.html
Hours of Operation:
Open Daily 9:00 am to 5:00 p.m.

**THE OLDE PINK HOUSE
RESTAURANT**
23 Abercorn Street
Savannah, GA 31401
(912) 232-4286
www.plantersinnsavannah.com
Hours of Operation:
Monday 5 p.m. to 10:30 p.m.
Tues.–Thurs. 11a.m.–2:30 p.m., 5–10:30 p.m.
Friday–Sat. 11a.m.–2:30 p.m., 5–11:00 p.m.
Sunday 5 p.m. to 10:30 p.m.

**THE PIRATE'S HOUSE
RESTAURANT**
20 East Broad Street
Savannah, GA 31401
www.thepirateshouse.com
Hours of Operation:
Monday to Thursday 11 a.m. to 9:30 p.m.
Friday to Saturday 11 a.m. to 10 p.m.
Sunday 11 a.m. to 9:30 p.m.

**SAVANNAH VISITOR'S CENTER AND
SAVANNAH HISTORY MUSEUM**
301 MLK Jr. Boulevard
Savannah, GA 31401
(912) 944-0455
www.visitsavannah.com/Info-and-Help/
Visitor-Center-Locations.aspx
Hours of Operation:
Monday to Sunday 9 a.m. to 5:30 p.m.
Museum Costs:
$8.50 for adults
$6.50 for students

**THE SIEGE OF SAVANNAH
BATTLEFIELD SITE (BATTLEFIELD
PARK)**
*On the corner of Louisville and MLK Jr.
Boulevard between the Visitor's Center and
the Roundhouse Railroad Museum.*
(912) 651-6825
Open daily. Closes at dusk.
General Admission: Free for visitors
Guided tours and programs are available.
Fees may apply.

THE SORREL-WEED HOUSE
6 West Harris Street
Savannah, GA 31401
(912) 257-2223
www.sorrelweedhouse.com
Daily daytime history tours and nightly
ghost tours.

BIBLIOGRAPHY

Auerbach, Loyd. *ESP, Hauntings, and Poltergeists: A Parapsychologist's Handbook*. New York, NY: Warner Books, 1987.

Berendt, John. *Midnight in the Garden of Good and Evil*. New York, NY: Random House Publishing, 1994.

Caskey, James. *Haunted Savannah: America's Most Spectral City*. Savannah, GA: Subtext Publishing, 2013.

Caskey, James. *Haunted Savannah: The Official Guidebook to Savannah Haunted History Tour*. Savannah, GA: Bonaventure Books, 2012.

Cobb, Al. *Savannah's Ghosts*. Atglen, PA: Schiffer Publishing, 2007.

Cook, Thomas H. *Blood Echoes: The Infamous Alday Mass Murder and Its Aftermath*. London, England: Penguin Group Publishing, 1993.

Coulter, E. Morton. *Wormsloe: Two Centuries of a Georgia Family*. Athens, GA: The University of Georgia Press, 1955.

Davis, Burke. *Sherman's March: The First Full-Length Narrative of General William T. Sherman's Devastating March*. New York, NY: Vintage Publishing, 1980.

Dunn, Ryan. *Savannah's Afterlife: True Tales of a Paranormal Investigator*. Atglen, PA: Schiffer Publishing, 2014.

Durham, Roger S. *The Blues in Gray: The Civil War Journal of William Daniel Dixon and the Republican Blues Daybook*. Knoxville, TN: The University of Tennessee Press, 2001.

Estep, Sarah. *Voices of Eternity*. New York, NY: Fawcett Publishing, 1988.

"From Savannah." *Columbian Centinel* (November 14, 1811), Boston, MA.

Gaston, Joseph. *A History and Genealogy of the Habersham Family*. London, England: Forgotten Books, 2015.

Grant, H. Roger. *Rails Through the Wiregrass: A History of the Georgia and Florida Railroad*. Dekalb, IL: Northern Illinois University Press, 2006.

Guiley, Rosemary Ellen. *The Encyclopedia of Demons and Demonology*. New York, NY: Checkmark Books, 2009.

Guiley, Rosemary Ellen. *The Encyclopedia of Ghosts and Spirits*. New York, NY: Checkmark Books, 1992.

Hanson, Robert H. *History of the Georgia Railroad*. Johnson City, TN: Overmountain Press, 1996.

Holzer, Hans. *Ghosts: True Encounters with the World Beyond*. Chicago: Black Dog and Leventhal Publishers, 1988.

Hough, Franklin Benjamin. *The Siege of Savannah: By the Combined American and French Forces, Under the Command of General Lincoln and the Count d'Estaing, in the Autumn of 1779.* Albany, NY: J. Munsell and Sons Publishing,1866.

Jones, Charles Colcock. *The Siege of Savannah: In 1779, as described in two contemporaneous journals of French officers in the fleet of Count d'Estaing.* Albany, NY: J. Munsell and Sons Publishing, 1874.

Keyes, Pam. *The Burning of the Vengeance and the Franchise at Savannah in 1811.* Galveston, TX: The Lafitte Society, 2008.

King, Spencer B. *Ebb Tide; As Seen through the Diary of Josephine Clay Habersham, 1863.* Athens, GA: University of Georgia Press, 1958.

Klacsmann, Karen Towers. *New Georgia Encyclopedia–William O. Golding.* Georgia: New Georgia Encyclopedia, 2008. http://www.georgiaencyclopedia.org/articles/arts-culture/william-o-golding-1874-1943.

Konstam, Dr. Angus. *The History of Pirates.* Guilford, CT: The Globe Pequot Press, 2002.

Konstam, Dr. Angus. *Piracy: The Complete History.* Oxford, England: Osprey Publishing, 2008.

Kornweibel Jr., Theodore. *Railroads in the African-American Experience: A Photographic Journey.* Baltimore, MD: John Hopkins University Press, 2010.

Lambert, Frank. "'Father against Son, and Son against Father': The Habershams of Georgia and the American Revolution." *Georgia Historical Quarterly* 84 (Spring 2000).

Lethbridge, Thomas Charles. *Ghost and Ghoul: An Archaeologists Account of his Personal Experiences with the Supernatural.* Doubleday & Company, 1962.

Maclay, Edgar Stanton. *A History of American Privateers.* Charleston, SC: Nabu Press, 2010.

Marsh, Carole. *Tomochichi: Chief of the Yamacraws, Friend of Savannah.* Peachtree City, GA: Gallopade International, 2005.

McConville, Sean. *Irish Political Prisoners 1848–1922: Theatres of War.* Florence, KY: Routledge Publishing, 2005.

McIlvenna, Noeleen. *The Short Life of Free Georgia: Class and Slavery in the Colonial South.* Chapel Hill, NC: The University of North Carolina Press, 2015.

OR Series 1, Volume 6, Chapter 15. *Correspondence, orders, and returns relating to operations on the coast of South Carolina, Georgia, and middle and East Florida from August 21, 1861, to April 11, 1862.* Savannah, GA, November 27, 1861, Capt. T. A. Washington to Assistant Adjutant General

Postell, Charles. *Dead Man Coming: A True Account of Carl Isaac's Trail of Murder.* Albany, GA: Network Publications, 1983.

Russell, Preston and Barbara Hines. *Savannah: A History of Her People Since 1733.* Savannah, GA: Frederic C. Beil, 2002.

Stevenson, Robert Louis. *Treasure Island.* London, England: Ladybird Books Ltd., reprinted 1999.

Steward, Theophilus Gould. *How the Black St. Domingo Legion Saved the Patriot Army in the Siege of Savannah, 1779.* Washington, DC: The Academy, 1899.

Todd, Helen. *Tomochichi.* Cary, NC: Cherokee Publishing Company, 2005.

Warren, Ed and Lorraine with Gerald Daniel Brittle. *The Demonologist.* Englewood Cliffs, NJ: Prentice-Hall, 1980.

Warren, Ed and Lorraine with Robert David Chase. *Ghost Hunters.* New York, NY: St. Martin's Paperbacks, 1989.

Warren, Mary Bondurant. *The First Settlers (1733–1740) (British Georgia).* Berwyn Heights, MD: Heritage Papers, 2015.

Weeks, Carla Ramsey. *The Sorrels of Savannah: Life on Madison Square and Beyond.* Parker, CO: Outskirts Press, 2009.

Young, Jeffrey Robert. *Slavery in Antebellum Georgia.* Georgia State University, 2003.

Ryan Dunn, along with his wife Kim, owns and operates the Savannah Ghost Research Society, which they founded in 2010. They also own Afterlife Tours, a walking ghost tour that features real paranormal evidence from their team's findings. They have been featured on A&E Biography's *My Ghost Story: Caught on Camera*, SyFy Channel's *Paranormal Witness*, CMT's *Party Down South*, as well as other networks. They also have their own television show entitled *Spooky Town* with WJCL-ABC News and Fox News 28 here in Savannah. The Dunns live in a haunted house in Savannah's historic district with their two daughters, Jennifer and Addison, along with their son, an English Bulldog named Griswold.